The Masai Language; Grammatical Notes
Together With a Vocabulary

THE MASAI LANGUAGE

London: C. J. CLAY AND SONS,
CAMBRIDGE UNIVERSITY PRESS WAREHOUSE,
AVE MARIA LANE

Glasgow 50, WELLINGTON STREET.

Leipzig F A BROCKHAUS
New York. THE MACMILLAN COMPANY
Bombay. E SEYMOUR HALE

THE MASAI LANGUAGE

GRAMMATICAL NOTES

TOGETHER WITH A

VOCABULARY

COMPILED BY

HILDEGARDE HINDE

CAMBRIDGE:

AT THE UNIVERSITY PRESS.

1901

𝕮𝖆𝖒𝖇𝖗𝖎𝖉𝖌𝖊.

PRINTED BY J. AND C. F. CLAY,

AT THE UNIVERSITY PRESS

PREFACE.

THE following small work on the Masai language was compiled by me during two years spent among the Masai people What I learnt was learnt directly from the Masai, and with no middleman in the way of Swahili or other native interpreters My excuse for undertaking a work of this description, without the special philological qualifications, is that I could converse freely with, and be fully understood by, any Masai, and that I could also well understand any Masai either talking to me or among themselves.

As my methods of learning and construing the language were not scientific but natural (if the contradistinction may be used), they may perhaps prove of some interest During the first few weeks among the Masai I could not even hear sufficiently what they said to be able to write down anything intelligible, and my own attempts at saying a few words were equally unintelligible to them. Since I was familiar with Swahili at the time it is improbable that this inability to hear or pronounce Masai should be ascribed to the fact that it is an African language. It is far more likely that the real difficulties of the language, intonation and accentuation, were hindering me, as Masai is undoubtedly difficult of pronunciation, construction and expression. When I was able to say a few words or sentences fairly correctly, I used them to every Masai I saw, and when they were said so that they were understood by a variety of people without hesitation I considered them correct. What one individual told me I told the next, and *vice versa*, thus correcting and recorrecting what I had originally written The difficulties of forming rules—since it was, of course, impossible to convey any idea of grammar to the Masai themselves—I solved by making a large number of sentences all similarly constructed: if the Masai construction of these sentences proved similar (after having taken sufficient examples, say twenty or thirty) I concluded that I had the necessary evidence on which to base a rule. It will be readily understood that the deductions arrived at by these methods were adequate to supply the small number of grammatical rules contained in the following pages.

Two attempts only have previously been made at classifying Masai The first is Ehrhardt's vocabulary (Wurtemburg, 1857), which contains some 1000 words. To this no grammatical rules are appended, and since Krapf states in the preface to the vocabulary that Ehrhardt learnt all he knew of Masai from Swahílis at the coast, it is natural he should have fallen into the error of treating and writing Masai as a Bantu language, *ie* a language of prefixes. Sir H H Johnston's vocabulary and notes on the Masai language, contained in the *Kilima Njaro Expedition*, are more ambitious than Ehrhardt's small volume, though he has evidently based his theories of the formation of the language on Ehrhardt's work That Sir H H. Johnston had also no opportunity of conversing directly with wild Masai he himself testifies The few Masai warriors whom he encountered at Mandara's court, and while he was actually travelling, he could only speak with through an interpreter, and the Wa-kwavi—from whom he learnt what he knew of the language—are not recognized by the wild Masai as members of their community. Sir H. H. Johnston states that the Wa-kwavi (their very name has been made Bantu) have intermarried with Bantus of all sorts; and it therefore follows that their language will probably have adopted many words other than Masai, and that the construction is likely to have been altered to that of the peoples among whom they live. I must take exception to the writing of Masai as employed both by Ehrhardt and Sir H H. Johnston. Though it is quite possible that originally the first syllables of Masai words denoted the gender, it is now equally impossible to write or treat of these words as separable from the first syllable. By so doing the language is converted into a language of prefixes, and a wrong interpretation is put on the words, since they are senseless and unintelligible if used without the first syllables. As inanimate objects are all neuter, and all animals (with the exception of cow, sheep, goat and donkey—the domestic animals of the Masai) are both masculine and feminine, the theory that *ol* is representative of the masculine gender and *n* or *en* of the feminine, can hardly hold good for example, *oridia* is equally dog or bitch, *orrgenoss* is equally a male or female crocodile, *mparnass* is equally a male or female duyker, *nottorrangi* is either a male or a female chameleon. What further bears out the theory that the current signification, of these first syllables, at any rate, is *not* denominative of gender, is the fact that "father" in Masai is *baba*, and "mother" *yeyu*, neither of these important words commencing with the gender prefix.

It seems, for various reasons, improbable that the Masai first syllables can be regarded by the Masai themselves as indicative of gender. Their distinction between male and female is very marked, the female being regarded as quite inferior. and bearing out this hypothesis Sir H H. Johnston says:—"masculine *ol* may be taken as meaning strong, big, masculine. .... The article *en* is mainly feminine in its significance, but it also gives a diminutive, depreciatory, weakened, playful, or affectionate character to the word it

precedes" (the *Kilima Njaro Expedition*, pages 455, 456).
It is unlikely that such important words as $\left.\begin{array}{l}\text{God}\\ \text{rain}\end{array}\right\} = ngai,$
fire = *ngima*, food = *nda*, country = *ngop*, day or sun = *ngolong*,
forest = *endim*, gun = *endiul*, meat = *engeringu*, game = *ngwess*,
grass = *engojeta*, etc., etc. should denote the feminine gender.
But according to Sir H. H. Johnston's theory this follows
unless they can be considered as representative of the
characteristics enumerated   The examples indicated should
sufficiently prove that the Masai significance of these first
syllables is not that suggested by Sir H. H. Johnston

I therefore consider the spelling of words as follows:
foot = ngaju, *en* (instead of *engeju*); donkey = sigira, *os*;
elephant = dome, *ol*; arm = gaina, *en*,—is wrong, and in no
way descriptive of the language, or indicated by it

Since the first syllable of Masai words must therefore be
regarded as almost invariably unchangeable, and as forming
part of the word itself, it seems inaccurate even to call it a
prefix. In Bantu languages one word is capable of having
a variety of prefixes attached to it, as for example. good =
-zuri *mzuri*, *mazuri*, *wazuri*, *vizuri*, *kizuri*   Here, in the
first instance, the root of the word is given with a dash
preceding it, since it is impossible to indicate the necessary
prefix unless the noun qualified is known. But the writing
of Masai words in this manner is alien to the structure of
the language   For example the word "good" (*sidai*) in
Masai is used for nouns of all denominations:

        sidai orlaiyon = a good boy,
        sidai engitok = a good woman,
        sidai ngishu = good cattle,
        sidai ngaji = a good house,
        sidai nda = good food,
        sidai orldia = a good dog

The verbs should surely be written in the infinitive or

the imperative. The roots, as given by Sir H. H. Johnston, convey little idea of the words intended to be represented by them, and can never be used conversationally in these forms I must also disagree with his placing the personal pronoun before the verbs when they are conjugated. I have carefully conjugated and studied over 70 verbs, and in one case only—the verb "to bring"—do the personal pronouns precede the verb all through In a great many verbs the abbreviations of "I" and "thou"—*a* or *i*—are used preceding the verbs, but the rest of the verb is usually conjugated with the pronouns following the verb Most frequently only the first person singular takes the abbreviation and precedes the verb.

ERRATA.

P. viii. par 2

For ngaju, *en* read gaju, *en*

P. ix   Read

.. in one case only—the verb "to bring"—do the personal pronouns ever precede the verb all through in this instance they would appear to precede or follow the verb optionally, and either form may be considered correct.

British East Africa, 1900.

M. G.   *b*

precedes" (the *Kilima Njaro Expedition*, pages 455, 456).
It is unlikely that such important words as ${}^{\text{God}}_{\text{rain}} \} = ngai,$
fire = *ngima*, food = *nda*, country = *ngop*, day or sun = *ngolong*,
forest = *endim*, gun = *endiul*, meat = *engeringu*, game = *ngwess*,
grass = *engojeta*, etc., etc should denote the feminine gender.
But according to Sir H. H. Johnston's theory this follows
unless they can be considered as representative of the
characteristics enumerated   The examples indicated should
sufficiently prove that the Masai significance of these first
syllables is not that suggested by Sir H H. Johnston.

· · · · consider the spelling of words as follows:

the language.   · · · · · ,
Masai is used for nouns of all denominations .

        sidai oilaiyon = a good boy,
        sidai engitok = a good woman,
        sidai ngishu   = good cattle,
        sidai ngaji   = a good house,
        sidai nda   = good food,
        sidai orldia   = a good dog

The verbs should surely be written in the infinitive or

the imperative   The roots, as given by Sir H. H. Johnston, convey little idea of the words intended to be represented by them, and can never be used conversationally in these forms. I must also disagree with his placing the personal pronoun before the verbs when they are conjugated. I have carefully conjugated and studied over 70 verbs, and in one case only—the verb "to bring"—do the personal pronouns precede the verb all through   In a great many verbs the abbreviations of "I" and "thou"—a or i—are used preceding the verbs, but the rest of the verb is usually conjugated with the pronouns following the verb. Most frequently only the first person singular takes the abbreviation and precedes the verb

Since Joseph Thompson made us acquainted with the Masai the word has invariably been pronounced with a hissing s. This is incorrect · the accent is very markedly on the first syllable—Māsai—and the s is not sharp

The difficulty of giving the right value to words in an unknown language has compelled me to adopt the long and the short accents   I have, however, done so as sparingly as possible, and only with regard to those words where the emphasis is so great that they would be unintelligible to the Masai if unaccented.

HILDEGARDE HINDE

British East Africa, 1900.

EDITOR'S NOTE.

Owing to Mrs Hinde's absence in Africa it was necessary to leave the revision of her proofs in other hands Any inaccuracies occurring in the text must, therefore, be ascribed to this fact

E C. M.

GRAMMATICAL RULES.

THERE are sounds in Masai corresponding to the following letters of the alphabet :

a b c d e g h i j k l m n o p r s t u w y

Besides these there are :

a   o   oi   u   sh   ss   rr   ai

The vowels are pronounced as in Italian and the consonants as in English.

The spelling adopted is, as far as possible, phonetic, and the accents merely the short and long. It is impossible to represent many words in Masai without accents, or to give any adequate idea of the pronunciation, without occasionally using the aspirate: as .—*oshiagi* = also, *ishigo* = better, etc, in which words the aspirate is distinctly audible.

b and *p* are almost similar in pronunciation, and are practically interchangeable, as are also *g* and *k*.

The voice is frequently sunk at the end of the word, and should the word end with a consonant it is sometimes so slightly pronounced that it is difficult to distinguish it.

The *r*, which I have written as *rr*, is very pronounced, being sounded with a marked burr

The *s* at the end of a word, and occasionally in the middle of a word, is sharply sounded as in hissing. This sound I have written as *ss*.

m and *n*, when commencing a word, and when followed by a consonant, are sounds of almost all African languages. The nearest approximation to their pronunciation is the slight sounding of the *m* in "mutter," and the *n* in "no":

they can neither be regarded as distinct syllables, nor must they be sounded as apart from the rest of the word.

The accent in Masai usually falls on the first syllable in words of two syllables, and in words of two or three syllables most usually on the second, but occasionally on the third. In words of more than three syllables the accent is usually on the second syllable. The accentuation is, however, not very regular, and in some words all the syllables are of equal value.

Abbreviation of words, and the cutting off of final vowels and even syllables is frequent and most confusing. In speaking, the words are not distinctly pronounced, but run on smoothly with no break, the syllables being often swallowed and the voice so sunk at intervals that it is difficult to catch all the words. The *liaison* is frequently used. The Masai have a strong feeling for euphony, and words are adapted and altered apparently for no other reason. Where two words, one ending and the other beginning with a vowel, follow one another, consonants (generally *n, k,* or *b*) are sometimes introduced, as ainyo *berora* = why sleep?

(1)   The Personal Pronouns are:

		Singular			*Plural*
1st person	I	nanu		we	iog or eeog
2nd ,,	thou	iye		you	ndai or iye
3rd ,,	{ he { she { it	nenye or ninyi		they	nenje or ninji

(2)   Questions are formed in Masai merely by using an interrogative tone of voice, as:

     I am ill   aemwi   Am I ill?   aemwi?

(3)   Negations are formed by prefixing the word "not," which is rendered by *meti* and its abbreviations *mer, me* and *m,* or by the words *ete, etwa, etu*

Meti is seldom used in full in conjunction with other words

Mer is used, evidently for the sake of euphony, before words beginning with a consonant, except before those beginning with an *s*: for these *me* is used. *m* is used for words beginning with a vowel.

Not bad	mer torono	Not milk	mer gule
Not good	me sidai	Not large	me sabuk
I do not want	maiu	I do not know	maiulu
I am not going	etwaolo	He will not bring	eteaw
	I am not tired	eteanawri	

(4) There are no conjunctions in Masai "And" is simply omitted, as:

The dog and cat	orldia embarrie (literally dog, cat)
The man and woman	eltungana engitok (man, woman)

O or *oi* are occasionally inserted between words supposed to be connected with a conjunction, but this is probably for the sake of euphony, as in most instances the final vowel of the first word is dropped, as · you and I = *nan oiye*, instead of *nanu iye*; he and you = *neny oiye*, instead of *nenye iye*. It must be admitted that in both these instances the altered form is the more euphonious

For the prepositions "with" and "for" there appear to be no words at all.

The preposition "in" (*atwa*) always precedes the noun it governs.

atwa ngaji	= in the house
atwa ngoshogi	= in the stomach
atwa engang	= in the kraal

(5) There are neither definite nor indefinite articles in Masai

(6) There are three genders in Masai: masculine, feminine and neuter.

The same word is used for male and female animals, with the exception of. sheep, goat, ass, cow, which have a different word for the male and female

All inanimate objects are neuter.

(7) Adjectives in Masai are invariable, and are only altered for the sake of euphony: when, for example, an adjective commencing with a vowel follows a substantive ending with a vowel, it may, under these circumstances, take a consonant preceding the vowel, as :

Red cloth	Hot water
engela kenyuki	ngare naii ogua

(8) The place of the adjective is undefined. it may either precede or follow the substantive, as :

A long house	A black goat
ēido ngāiji	ndaii nārok

(9) The numeral adjectives always follow the substantive, and usually end the sentence :

I see a hundred cows
Arradua ngishu īip.

(10) The numeral adjectives are as follows ·

1 = nabu
2   ari *or* are
3   ūni
4   ungwun
5   miet
6   elle
7   nabishāna
8   issiet
9   nawdu *or* endōiroi
10   tomon
11   tomon obbo
12   tomon are
13   tomon ogūni

14 = tomon ungwun
15   tomon oimiet
16   tomon oiille
17   tomon nabishāna
18   tomon oissiet
19   tomon nawdo
20   tigitum
21   tigitum obbo
30   ossom
31   ossom obbo
40   arrtam
41   arrtam obbo
50   orrnom
51   orinom obbo
60 = ip (which equals our 100. The Masai count in
       sixties, and a company of warriors is composed
       of 60 men)
Two sixties = ip ari
First = tangasamo
Last = korom.

Like all primitive peoples the Masai count on their
fingers The closed fist represents 5, the two closed fists 10.
For higher numbers the fists are moved up and down until
the multiplication has been made. To represent 60, or any
higher figure, the fingers of one hand are snapped, but if the
number be very large the fingers of both hands are snapped
several times.

(11) Adjectives are capable of declension, and follow
the same rules as verbs They do not alter according to
gender, but almost invariably for the sake of euphony:
occasionally they take the same plural as the noun they
qualify. In some instances the auxiliary verb is in no way
represented, the adjective only being used with the personal

pronouns In other instances the auxiliary verb is used, the
adjective in both instances being declined.

I am ill	aemwi
Thou ait ill	emwciye
He she or it is ill	emwenenje
We are ill	kemwesiog
You aie ill	emwewe ndai
They are ill	ana imwiwi
I am tiied	aranawei
Thou art tired	atanauriiye
He she or it is tircd	kerenauie nenye
We are tired	keternauiiawdisiog
You aie tiied	anaura ndai
They are tired	keianauia ata ncnje
I am well	arabiēio
Thou ait well	eiaiiyebiēio
He she oi it is well	biero ossenenje
Wc aie well	heia biot
You aie well	eraiandai biot
They aie well •	aibio nenje

(12) The possessive adjective always follows the noun.
The various words for each adjective aie used for the sake
of euphony ·

Oui boma	engang*ang*
Our cows	ngishu*nng*
My fathei	baba *lai*
My hand	ngaiin*ai*

my	*lai, elai* or *ai*	oui	*enãang, nnq, oog*
thine	*eniio*	your	*eninyi, nyn, liiyi*
his / hers / its	*enenye, eno*	their	*ãasho, ejanggurr, enje*

(13) All verbs in Masai are conjugated, and with a certain
degree of regularity. In some cases the abbreviations of "I"
and "thou" (*a* or *i*) are used preceding the verb, but almost
invariably the pronoun follows the verb, which commences

the sentence. All negatives and interrogatives, however, precede the verbs

I know	I do not know	What are you doing?
aiulu	*maiulu*	*ainyo endobera* ?

The infinitive mood always commences with an *n* : frequently this *n* is simply prefixed to the first person singular, though the larger number of infinitives merely bear some general resemblance to the verb. Where the infinitive singular is formed by prefixing an *n* to the first person singular, the second and third persons singular also usually take an *n* instead of using the first person, as ·

to go	*nalo*	1st person
	nilo	2nd person
	nelo	3rd person
to come	*nalotu*	1st person
	nelotu	2nd and 3rd persons

The persons plural all use one word, though this is often distinct from the singular. In cases where the infinitive simply bears a general resemblance to the verb, all the persons singular use this word. In many verbs the singular and plural have slightly different infinitives, though both invariably have the *n* prefix, as

	Singular	*Plural*
to cut	*nadung*	*negidung*
to catch	*nebong*	*negibong*
to bathe	*naisoja*	*negasoja*

(14) The present and future tenses of verbs are alike. The past tense is formed by prefixing the word *edeba* (finished) to the verb, which thus becomes an auxiliary verb.

(15) The verbs " to be " and " to have " always precede the noun. all other verbs follow it The past tenses of these two verbs, if existent, are not in general use. The usual

method of expressing their past tense is by using the present
tense with an adverb denoting time, as:

I am yesterday   I have a cow last night
          I am in Naivasha last moon.

The present tense of " to be " is :

Singular		Plural	
I am	*aad, ara* or *a*	we are	*kera* or *era iog*
thou art	*eraiiye, eata* or *e*	you are	*eraia* or *eraiandai*
he			
she is	*eerda eera* or *ata nenye*	they are	*ana* or *eranenje* or *weji*
it			

The present tense of "to have" is exactly the same as the
present tense of " to be " · there is no distinction between
the two verbs.

(16) There is an imperative mood, both singular and
plural, to all verbs. The imperative singular almost invariably commences with *t* and the plural with *en* : both
usually resemble the verb. Examples :

		Imp Sing	Imp Plural
I sing	airany	tananya	endairain
I climb	atakedu	tagedo	endagedi
I break	agil nanu	tegella	endegi
I say	etejo nanu	toojo	endojo

(17) Nouns in Masai form their plurals by affixes,
though occasionally the middle syllables of the word may
also be altered.

(18) There are nine regular methods of forming the
plural , they are as follows .

		Sing	Plural	
(1)	i or oi or ni	engela	engelani	= clothes
		ndap	ndapi	= hand
		orlörio	orlörioi	= goat (male)
(2)	a or ia	oldulet	olduleta	= bottle
		essurutie	essorudia	= earring
		essondai	essondä	= wall

		Sing	*Plural*	
(3)	u, tu	ɩngobɩrr	ɩngobɩrru	= feather
		emurrt	emurrtu	= neck
		oldonуi	elōmtu	= skɩn
(4)	n, in	ossesɩ	essessɩn	= body
		ōrgenoss	ergenossɩn	= crocodɩle
		mbarrda	mbaɩrdan	= horse
(5)	k, ak, ok	ngorraɩon	ngorroɩok	= woman
		emoworr	mowarrak	= horn
		orlāmonon	lamonok	= beggar
(6)	g	ngaɩna	ngaɩeg	= arm
		ndāɾɩdɩgɩ	ndāɾɩdig	= bɩrd
(7)	r or rr	ngera	ngerr	= sheep
		emossori	emossoɩr	= egg
		endōlu	endōluer	= axe
(8)	o	olashɩ	olasho	= calf
		endōlɩt	endōlo	= marrow
(9)	t	ollogurrto	ollogurrt	= caterpillar
		engumoru	engumurrt	= hole
		engɩas	engɩaset	= work

(19) Two words—mother and twig—form their plurals by prefixes:

yeyu	noɩyeyu
loom	eloom

I have found no trace of nouns forming their plurals with the prefixes *ku* or *k*.

(20) A large number of nouns form their plurals quite irregularly; some alter the first syllable or middle syllables, but in many instances the whole word is changed:

	Sing	*Plural*
tɩck	oɩromashere	ellemasher
dance	ɩngɩrɩgɩra	maɩguraɩa
hippopotamus	ollomagaw	errmagawl
breast	orrɩgena	ellgɩē
mark	orrborrnoto	ɩrrgonot
chaɩr	oloɩɩika	lorrɩgaɩshi
kudu	emālo	mɩggɩbɩ

(21)   Some nouns are alike both in singular and plural

sun or suns	ngolong
beard or beards	oitimunyi
flea or fleas	loisusu
fire or fires	ngima
father or fathers	baba

(22)   When used in conjunction with verbs of negation nouns are capable of conjugation .

I have not anything	maadatoki
Thou hast not anything	mieraisietoki
He she or it has not anything	meerasenenye
We have not anything	mieraiog
You have not anything	mierarasendai
They have not anything	keeia nenje

(23)   The interrogatives "why" and "what" (*ainyo*) when preceding a noun, pronoun, adjective or verb, insert *b, be,* or *ba* between the two words, as · why sleep ? *ainyo berora ?* The entire interrogative may be omitted, with the exception of the final *o,* and written *oberora,* or even further abbreviated to *oba.*

Why go '	ainyo *b*elo '
Why good ?	ainyo *ba*sidai ?
Why drink ?	ainyo *b*eiōk ?

VERBS.

Present or Future Tense   *Imperative Mood*

Infinitive of **to go** =
$$\begin{cases} \textbf{nalo} \\ \textbf{nillo} \\ \textbf{nello} \\ \textbf{nigibu} \text{ (plural)} \end{cases} \text{ (singular)}$$

I go or will go	alo nanu		
Thou goest or wilt go	illoiye	Go thou	shomo
He she or it goes or will go	kello nenye		
We go or will go	kibuuyook		
You go or will go	e-homo ndai	Go you	anshom or mããbe
They go or will go	kebo nenje		

Infinitive of **to see** =
$$\begin{cases} \textbf{nadol} \text{ (singular)} \\ \textbf{negidol} \text{ (plural)} \end{cases}$$

I see or will see	ariadua nanu		
Thou seest or wilt see	etaduai iye	See thou	etadua
He she or it sees or will see	etadua nenye		
We see or will see	kiiaduiog		
You see or will see	ertadua ndai	See you	etaduã
They see or will see	anaetadua		

Infinitive of **to want** =
$$\begin{cases} \textbf{naiyu} \\ \textbf{niyu} \\ \textbf{neyu} \\ \textbf{negiaiu} \text{ (plural)} \end{cases} \text{ (singular)}$$

I want or shall want	aiyu nanu		
Thou wantest or shalt want	iyu iye	Want thou	toomono
He she or it wants or will want	keyu or eyu nenye		
We want or shall want	kiyu iog		
You want or will want	ivu ndai	Want ye	tromono
They want or shall want	keyu nenji		

Present or Future Tense   *Imperative Mood*

Infinitive of **to bring** = $\begin{cases} \text{naiau} \\ \text{niyau} \\ \text{neyau} \\ \text{negiau} \end{cases}$ (singular) (plural)

I bring or will bring	aiau nanu	
Thou bringest or wilt bring	yau iye	Bring thou iau
He she or it brings or will bring	eyau nenye	
We bring or will bring	iognaiau	
You bring or will bring	ndainaiau	Bring ye eau
They bring or will bring	anaiau	

Infinitive of **to return** = $\begin{cases} \text{narrinyo (singular)} \\ \text{nigurinyo (plural)} \end{cases}$

I return or will return	arrinyo nanu	
Thou returnest or wilt return	torrinyo iye	Return thou toirinyoi
He she or it returns or will return	errorinyi	
We return or will return	keirinyoi yok	
You return or will return	irinyoiyo ndai	Return ye torrininyi
They return or will return	anairrinyu	

Infinitive of **to hear** = $\begin{cases} \text{naning (singular)} \\ \text{negining (plural)} \end{cases}$

I hear or will hear	atoringu	
Thou hearest or wilt hear	itoringu	Hear thou toringu
He she or it hears or will hear	kerroninonginye	
We hear or will hear	kerroninong ossiog	
You hear or will hear	etonginong ndai	Hear ye endonyin
They hear or will hear	kerroninonginje	

Infinitive of **to come** = $\begin{cases} \text{nalotu} \\ \text{nilotu} \\ \text{neloto} \\ \text{negibon} \end{cases}$ (singular) (plural)

I come or will come	ālotu	
Thou comest or wilt come	elotu iye	Come thou woo
He she or it comes or will come	elotu nenye	
We come or will come	kiboniog	
You come or will come	iētu ndai	Come ye ñotu or ōō
They come or will come	kietuaninji	

Present or Future Tense   *Imperative Mood*

Infinitive of **to make** = $\begin{cases}\text{naitobera (singular)}\\ \text{negindoberr (plural)}\end{cases}$

I make or will make	airoberr nanu		
Thou makest or wilt make	endoberiye	Make thou	endobera
He she or it makes or will make	ketoberr ninyi		
We make or will make	kindoberra yōōg		
You make or will make	endobera ndai	Make ye	kitobera
They make or will make	kitoberr ninji		

Infinitive of **to know** = $\begin{cases}\text{naiulu (singular)}\\ \text{negiolog (plural)}\end{cases}$

I know or shall know	nanu naiulu		
Thou knowest or wilt know	iye naiulu	Know thou	aiulu
He she or it knows or will know	enlu nenye		
We know or shall know	kiolo iog		
You know or will know	eololo ndai	Know ye	aiuloito
They know or will know	eolonenje		

Infinitive of **to love** = $\begin{cases}\text{nanyorr (singular)}\\ \text{negenyorr (plural)}\end{cases}$

I love or will love	anyoir nanu		
Thou lovest or wilt love	enyori iye	Love thou	tonyorra
He she or it loves or will love	kenyori nenye		
We love or will love	envossiyog		
You love or will love	kenyoii ndai	Love ye	tonyorr
They love or will love	kenyori ninji		

Infinitive of **to give** = $\begin{cases}\text{nenjog or naisho (singular)}\\ \text{neginjog (plural)}\end{cases}$

I give or will give	aiisho nanu		
Thou givest or wilt give	injŏğ iye	Give thou	enjŏŏğ
He she or it gives or will give	ejenjŏğenenye		
We give or will give	kenjŏğ iog		
You give or will give	enjoshŏğ ndai	Give ye	enjŏŏğ ninji
They give or will give	ki-hoğ eninji		

Present or Future Tense   *Imperative Mood*

Infinitive of **to kill** = $\begin{cases} \text{naying or neying (singular)} \\ \text{negiying (plural)} \end{cases}$

I kill or will kill	aiyin nanu		
Thou killest or wilt kill	iyen iye	Kill thou	teyunga
He she or it kills or will kill	keyeng nenye		
We kill or will kill	kiyeng siog		
You kill or will kill	keyeng ndai	Kill ye	endeyeng
They kill or will kill	keyeng ninji		

Infinitive of **to carry** = $\begin{cases} \text{nanab or naier (singular)} \\ \text{negeer (plural)} \end{cases}$

I carry or will carry	aiya nanu		
Thou carriest or wilt carry	$\begin{cases} \text{tanaba iye} \\ \text{eyaiyan iye} \end{cases}$	Carry thou	$\begin{cases} \text{tanabo} \\ \text{yaua iye} \end{cases}$
He she or it carries or will carry	$\begin{cases} \text{kenaba nenye} \\ \text{ewadu nenye} \end{cases}$		
We carry or will carry	keyau iōg		
You carry or will carry	yai ndai	Carry ye	ewāretar
They carry or will carry	keai ninyi		

Infinitive of **to finish** = $\begin{cases} \text{naideba (singular)} \\ \text{negendeb (plural)} \end{cases}$

I finish or will finish	aideba		
Thou finishest or wilt finish	edebaiye	Finish thou	idebi
He she or it finishes or will finish	edeba nenye		
We finish or will finish	kendeba iyog		
You finish or will finish	endeba ndai	Finish ye	endeba
They finish or will finish	edeba ninji		

Infinitive of **to fold** = $\begin{cases} \text{nagil or naien (singular)} \\ \text{negerred (plural)} \end{cases}$

I fold or will fold	agil		
Thou foldest or wilt fold	teredaiye	Fold thou	teena
He she or it folds or will fold	tereda nenye		
We fold or will fold	ketereda iyog		
You fold or will fold	eterera ndai	Fold ye	endēēn
They fold or will fold	eterida ninji		

Present or Future Tense   *Imperative Mood*

Infinitive of **to fly** = {nebirr or nebɪrri (singular)
{negibirr (plural)

I fly or will fly	aɪbidu		
Thou fliest or wilt fly	ɪbɪdoɪye	Fly thou	eeda
He she or it flies or will fly	kɪbɪdo nenye		
We fly or will fly	kɪbɪdo ɪyok		
You fly or will fly	embɪdo ndaɪ	Fly ye	eeda
They fly or will fly	ebɪdo nɪnɟi		

Infinitive of **to laugh** = {nakwenɪ (singular)
{nigigweni (plural)

I laugh or will laugh	atagwenɪa		
Thou laughest or wilt laugh	ɪgwen ɪye	Laugh thou	tagwenɪa
He she or it laughs or will laugh	katagwenɪa nɪnyi		
We laugh or will laugh	ketagwenɪa sɪog		
You laugh or will laugh	etagwenɪa ndaɪ	Laugh ye	tagwenɪa bōōgi
They laugh or will laugh	ketagwenɪa nɪnɟi		

Infinitive of **to cut** = {nadung (singular)
{negidung (plural)

I cut or will cut	atudung		
Thou cuttest or wilt cut	itudungoɪye	Cut thou	tudungu
He she or it cuts or will cut	ketudungu nenye		
We cut or will cut	ketudung ɪog		
You cut or will cut	ketudung ndaɪ	Cut ye	endudung
They cut or will cut	ketudungo nenɟe		

Infinitive of **to call** = {naibot or nēebot (singular)
{negɪnbot (plural)

I call or will call	aɪboto		
Thou callest or wilt call	emboto iye	Call thou	emboto
He she or it calls or will call	keboto nenye		
We call or will call	kɪmboto ɪog		
You call or will call	kɪmboto ndaɪ	Call ye	emboto
They call or will call	k.ɪɪboto ɪɪ.ɪɪ ;		

| *Present or Future Tense* | | *Imperative Mood* |

Infinitive of **to catch** = { nebong (singular) / negibong (plural)

I catch or will catch	aïbonğ		
Thou catchest or wilt catch	embongaiye	Catch thou	emboonga
He she or it catches or will catch	kebonga ninyi		
We catch or will catch	embongaiyog		
You catch or will catch	embonga ndai	Catch ye	emboonga
They catch or will catch	embonga ninji		

Infinitive of **to climb** = { naged (singular) / negiged (plural)

I climb or will climb	atakedu		
Thou climbest or wilt climb	iked iye	Climb thou	tagedo
He she or it climbs or will climb	karagedo nenye*		
We climb or will climb	karagedo siog		
You climb or will climb	karageda ndai	Climb ye	endagedi
They climb or will climb	kegede ninji		

Infinitive of **to buy** = { nainyangu or nenyong (singular) / neginyawng (plural)

I buy or will buy	ainyawngo		
Thou buyest or wilt buy	inyang iye	Buy thou	inyangu
He she or it buys or will buy	kemer nenye		
We buy or will buy	inyangu iog		
You buy or will buy	inyangu ndai	Buy ye	enyangu
They buy or will buy	inyangu nenje		

Infinitive of **to cook** = { naierishu or neyerr (singular) / negiyerr (plural)

I cook or will cook	aierishu		
Thou cookest or wilt cook	iryerishoiye	Cook thou	taiara
He she or it cooks or will cook	iryerisho nenye		
We cook or will cook	iryerishoiiog		
You cook or will cook	enaiyerisho	Cook ye	endaierishu
They cook or will cook	iryerisho ninji		

* In this instance karagedo can be spelt karakedo, the g and k being interchangeable.

Present or Future Tense   *Imperative Mood*

Infinitive of **to cry** = $\begin{cases}\textbf{naisherr (singular)}\\\textbf{negenjerr (plural)}\end{cases}$

I cry or will cry	aishera		
Thou criest or wilt cry	injeraiye	Cry thou	injēēra
He she or it cries or will cry	eisher nenye		
We cry or will cry	kinjera siog		
You cry or will cry	enai injeir	Cry ye	ēnjera
They cry or will cry	eshera ninji		

Infinitive of **to clean** = $\begin{cases}\textbf{naworr or neworr (singular)}\\\textbf{negiworr}\\\textbf{noor}\end{cases}\text{(plural)}$

I clean or will clean	aisoj nanu		
Thou cleanest or wilt clean	issōjī ye	Clean thou	essoja
He she or it cleans or will clean	kessōj ninyi		
We clean or will clean	kessojanog		
You clean or will clean	ana kessoj	Clean ye	essoja
They clean or will clean	essoj ninji		

Infinitive of **to bathe or wash** = $\begin{cases}\textbf{naisoja (singular)}\\\textbf{negasoja (plural)}\end{cases}$

I bathe or will bathe	aisoja		
Thou bathest or wilt bathe	essojai ye	Bathe thou	essojaiu
He she or it bathes or will bathe	kessoja nenye		
We bathe or will bathe	kessoja siog		
You bathe or will bathe	anakessoja	Bathe ye	essojana
They bathe or will bathe	essoja nenje		

Infinitive of **to wait** = $\begin{cases}\textbf{naanya (singular)}\\\textbf{neginanya (plural)}\end{cases}$

I wait or shall wait	aanyo		
Thou waitest or wilt wait	taanvoiye	Wait thou	ndaishu
He she or it waits or will wait	keainyo nenye		
We wait or will wait	tianyiyoog		
You wait or will wait	anagiaïno	Wait ye	endaendai
They wait or will wait	tianyo nenje		

Present or Future Tense   *Imperative Mood*

Infinitive of **to bite** = { **nawon** or **naawŏn** (singular)
{ **negiwon** (plural)

I bite or will bite	atoonyo		
Thou bitest or wilt bite	atoon iye	Bite thou	toonyo
He she or it bites or will bite	kawenenye		
We bite or will bite	kaweniog		
You bite or will bite	anakawan	Bite ye	endoonyn
They bite or will bite	kawanenje		

Infinitive of **to sleep** = { **nairora** or **nerora** (singular)
{ **negirora** (plural)

I sleep or will sleep	airora nanu		
Thou sleepest or wilt sleep	erora iye	Sleep thou	erorai
He she or it sleeps or will sleep	erora nenye		
We sleep or will sleep	erora iog		
You sleep or will sleep	erora ndai	Sleep ye	erraga
They sleep or will sleep	anagerora		

Infinitive of **to break** = { **nagil** or **negil** (singular)
{ **negegil** or **neerdan** (plural)

I break or will break	agil nanu		
Thou breakest or wilt break	tegelaiiye	Break thou	tegella
He she or it breaks or will break	kegel nenye		
We break or will break	kegel iog		
You break or will break	anai igil	Break ye	endegi
They break or will break	kegel nenje		

Infinitive of **to dig** = **nashid, neturr** or **nairem**

I dig or will dig	atur nanu		
Thou diggest or wilt dig	tuturuiye	Dig thou	irotuturu
He she or it digs or will dig	ketuturo ninyi		
We dig or will dig	ketuturo siog		
You dig or will dig	anagetu	Dig ye	ainshom en-dudu
They dig or will dig	eturrninji		

Present or Future Tense   *Imperative Mood*

Infinitive of **to build** = neegarr or nairau

I build or will build	aitwa		
Thou buildest or wilt build	endawi	Build thou	daisherdei
He she or it builds or will build	etaw ninyi		
We build or will build	kendaw iog		
You build or will build	anaiedaw	Build ye	endaishet
They build or will build	edaweninji		

Infinitive of **to fall** = nebarr or nabarada

I fall or shall fall	atabaradi		
Thou fallest or wilt fall	etabaiad iye	Fall thou	tabaraiaio
He she or it falls or will fall	etabaiadi ninyi		
We fall or shall fall	ketabaiadadiog		
You fall or will fall	etabaradadandai	Fall ye	tabaraiaio
They fall or will fall	enaketabaiada		

Infinitive of **to beg** = namon or niomon

I beg or will beg	monisho nanu		
Thou beggest or wilt beg	monisho iye	Beg thou	toomono
He she or it begs or will beg	monisho ninyi		
We beg or will beg	monisho iog		
You beg or will beg	monisho ndai	Beg ye	lãamonok
They beg or will beg	anakiomonisho		

Infinitive of **to blow** = { nerr or neenok (singular) / negenok (plural) }

I blow or will blow	togota nanu		
Thou blowest or wilt blow	togota iye	Blow thou	togota
He she or it blows or will blow	togotai nenye		
We blow or will blow	endokotiog		
You blow or will blow	endokotendai	Blow ye	endogot
They blow or will blow	endokotenenje		

2—2

Present or Future Tense   *Imperative Mood*

Infinitive of **to boil** = {naitokitok (singular)
negirri (plural)}

I boil or will boil	aitokitoki		
Thou boilest or wilt boil	etokitok iye	Boil thou	ēntokitoki
He she or it boils or will boil	etokitoki ninyi		
We boil or will boil	etokitoki siog		
You boil or will boil	etokitok ndai	Boil ye	ēntokitok
They boil or will boil	ketokitoki ninji		

Infinitive of **to bend** = {nerriu (singular)
negirriu (plural)}

I bend or will bend	togoiomaiyo		
Thou bendest or wilt bend	agoiroma iye	Bend thou	errogovu
He she or it bends or will bend	agoiroma nenye		
We bend or will bend	barragorramarra		
You bend or will bend	endogoiamari	Bend ye	errogoyu
They bend or will bend	kegorroma nenje		

Infinitive of **to eat** = {nanya (singular)
neginyanda (plural)}

I eat or will eat	anya nanu		
Thou eatest or wilt eat	kinya iye	Eat thou	enossa
He she or it eats or will eat	kenya nenye		
We eat or will eat	kenya siog		
You eat or will eat	kenya ndai	Eat ye	enossa
They eat or will eat	{kenya nenje, oō nenje, enosseje}		

Infinitive of **to drink** = nawok or niog

I drink or will drink	awok		
Thou drinkest or wilt drink	iok iye	Drink thou	toōgo
He she or it drinks or will drink	keyog nenye		
We drink or will drink	aiog iog		
You drink or will drink	ewogkiog ndai	Drink ye	endoōg
They drink or will drink	kewog nenje		

Present or Future Tense   *Imperative Mood*

$$\text{Infinitive of } \textbf{to tell} = \begin{cases} \textbf{najogi} \text{ (singular)} \\ \textbf{negijoogi} \text{ (plural)} \end{cases}$$

I tell or will tell	ajogi nanu		
Thou tellest or wilt tell	ijog iye	Tell thou	tiagi
He she or it tells or will tell	ejoge nenye		
We tell or will tell	kejog iog		
You tell or will tell	kejoginendai	Tell ye	tiagi
They tell or will tell	kejoginenje		

$$\text{Infinitive of } \textbf{to sing} = \begin{cases} \textbf{neeran} \text{ (singular)} \\ \textbf{negerran} \text{ (plural)} \end{cases}$$

I sing or will sing	ariany̆		
Thou singest or wilt sing	erran iye	Sing thou	tarranya
He she or it sings or will sing	kerranenye		
We sing or will sing	keteranassiog		
You sing or will sing	eterranyan ndai	Sing ye	endaiiain
They sing or will sing	kerrai nenje		

$$\text{Infinitive of } \textbf{to put} = \begin{cases} \textbf{nairagi} \text{ or } \textbf{nebi} \text{ (singular)} \\ \textbf{negiragi} \text{ (plural)} \end{cases}$$

I put or will put	eiagai nanu		
Thou puttest or wilt put	eiagiye	Put thou	erāgi
He she or it puts or will put	eiage nenye		
We put or will put	kerragissiog		
You put or will put	kerragai ndai	Put ye	eriagē
They put or will put	kerragai nenje		

$$\text{Infinitive of } \textbf{to sit} = \begin{cases} \textbf{nardon} \text{ (singular)} \\ \textbf{netornyi} \text{ (plural)} \end{cases}$$

I sit or will sit	ator nanu		
Thou sittest or wilt sit	toionaiye	Sit thou	toidona
He she or it sits or will sit	keroranya nenye		
We sit or will sit	kiton iog		
You sit or will sit	andaraian ndai	Sit ye	etordona
They sit or will sit	otonorto nenje		

Present or Future Tense   *Imperative Mood*

Infinitive of **to look** = { **naingora** or **neengorr** (singular)
{ **negengorr** (plural)

I look or will look	engor nanu		
Thou lookest or wilt look	engoraiye	Look thou	engoräii
He she or it looks or will look	engora nenye		
We look or will look	keyaw } siog kengoia }		
You look or will look	kengoia ndai	Look ye	engorä
They look or will look	kengera nenje		

Infinitive of **to spit** = { **nenortargi** (singular)
{ **neginortagi** (plural)

I spit or will spit	tonoitagi		
Thou spittest or wilt spit	etonoitagiye	Spit thou	tonoitaigi
He she or it spits or will spit	ketonoitag nenye		
We spit or will spit	kenotag iog		
You spit or will spit	enototargi ndai	Spit ye	tonoitargi
They spit or will spit	enototaigi nenje		

Infinitive of **to open** = { **nabol** or **nebol** (singular)
{ **negibol** (plural)

I open or will open	alag nanu		
Thou openest or wilt open	etalag iye	Open thou	{taala {tobollo
He she or it opens or will open	kalago nenye		
We open or will open	kelaguyoog		
You open or will open	elagalag ndai	Open ye	eudala
They open or will open	keralagu nenje		

Infinitive of **to shut** = { **naigen** (singular)
{ **nigingin** (plural)

I shut or will shut	āteena		
Thou shuttest or wilt shut	ēen iye	Shut thou	teena
He she or it shuts or will shut	ēenenye		
We shut or will shut	ēen iog		
You shut or will shut	ēen ndai	Shut ye	endeen
They shut or will shut	ēenenje		

Present or Future Tense   *Imperative Mood*

Infinitive of **to stand** = {naitashi (singular)
negendaishi (plural)}

I stand or will stand	aitashu		
Thou standest or wilt stand	endaishu iye	Stand thou	endaishu
He she or it stands or will stand	kedaishe nenye		
We stand or will stand	kendaishiniog		
You stand or will stand	endasheshendai	Stand ye	endäishu
They stand or will stand	edashe nenje		

Infinitive of **to pull** = {naiyeta (singular)
negiyetu (plural)}

I pull or will pull	aiyetu		
Thou pullest or wilt pull	teyeraiye	Pull thou	teyerai
He she or it pulls or will pull	teyeraiy nenye		
We pull or will pull	kierai iog		
You pull or will pull	eteryeraiyendai	Pull ye	endeyerai
They pull or will pull	eteiyeraiyenenje		

Infinitive of **to remove** = {naidaw or nadomo (singular)
negendaw (plural)}

I remove or will remove	adomo nanu		
Thou removest or wilt remove	idom iye	Remove thou	{todomo / endaw}
He she or it removes or will remove	edomo nenye		
We remove or will remove	edom iog		
You remove or will remove	endodom ndai	Remove ye	endodomo
They remove or will remove	kerdomo nenje		

Infinitive of **to dance** = {nengorran (singular)
negigorran (plural)}

I dance or will dance	aigurran		
Thou dancest or wilt dance	ingurran iye	Dance thou	ingurrana
He she or it dances or will dance	engurran nenye		
We dance or will dance	engurran iog		
You dance or will dance	engorran ndai	Dance ye	engurian
They dance or will dance	kegorran nenje		

Present or Future Tense   *Imperative Mood*

$$\text{Infinitive of } \textbf{to swear} = \begin{cases} \textbf{nadek} \\ \textbf{aadek} \\ \textbf{negedek} \end{cases} \begin{array}{l} \text{(singular)} \\ \\ \text{(plural)} \end{array}$$

I swear or will swear	amoir nanu		
Thou swearest or wilt swear	moir iye	Sweai thou	tamoro
He she or it swears or will swear	kemoii nenye		
We swear or will sweai	emoir iog		
You sweai or will swear	emorromoir ndai	Swear ye	tamoro
They sweai oi will swear	kemori nenje		

$$\text{Infinitive of } \textbf{to steal} = \begin{cases} \textbf{neberro} \text{ (singulai)} \\ \textbf{negibirro} \text{ (plural)} \end{cases}$$

I steal or will steal	atuborrishi		
Thou stealest or wilt steal	etuburiushoiye	Steal thou	tubuiioi
He she or it steals or will steal	etuburrushoi nenye		
We steal or will steal	ketubuirushi siog		
You steal or will steal	ketuburrisho ndai	Steal ye	endubuiioi
They steal or will steal	keburrisho nenje		

$$\text{Infinitive of } \textbf{to hunt} = \begin{cases} \textbf{nengorishu} \text{ (singulai)} \\ \textbf{negingorishu} \text{ (plural)} \end{cases}$$

I hunt oi will hunt	angoiisho		
Thou huntest or wilt hunt	engorishoiye	Hunt thou	angoiiisho
He she oi it hunts or will hunt	engorishoi nenye		
We hunt oi will hunt	kengoiishoi siog		
You hunt oi will hunt	engoiishoi ndai	Hunt ye	andangorr. isho
They hunt oi will hunt	engorishoi nenje		

Present or Future Tense   *Imperative Mood*

Infinitive of **to refuse** $=\begin{cases}\text{nian or ān (singular)}\\ \text{negian (plural)}\end{cases}$

I refuse or will refuse	aiin nanu		
Thou refusest or wilt refuse	een iye	Refuse thou	taanya
He she or it refuses or will refuse	keenenye		
We refuse or will refuse	kian siog		
You refuse or will refuse	iamandai	Refuse ye	endaān
They refuse or will refuse	keánenje		

Infinitive of **to forget** $=\begin{cases}\text{nariginu or ireginu (singular)}\\ \text{negeriginu (plural)}\end{cases}$

I forget or will forget	atorigini nanu		
Thou forgettest or wilt forget	ekitorigin iye	Forget thou	adorigin
He she or it forgets or will forget	ketorigine nenye		
We forget or will forget	etorigin iog		
You forget or will forget	etorigin ndai	Forget ye	adorigin
They forget or will forget	etorigine nenje		

Infinitive of **to run away** $=\begin{cases}\text{nilwaiyer (singular)}\\ \text{negilwaiyer (plural)}\end{cases}$

I run or will run away	aibiiriyu		
Thou runnest or wilt run away	imbirr iye	Run away thou embirriu	
He she or it runs or will run away	keburi nenye		
We run or will run away	embiretu ossiog		
You run or will run away	embirridi ndai	Run ye away	embirriu
They run or will run away	embirri nenje		

Infinitive of **to pour** $=\begin{cases}\text{nabeg (singular)}\\ \text{negibeg (plural)}\end{cases}$

I pour or will pour	aisuagi		
Thou pourest or wilt pour	essuag iye	Pour thou	tebega
He she or it pours or will pour	essuage nenye		
We pour or will pour	essuag issiog		
You pour or will pour	essuagi ndai	Pour ye	endebega
They pour or will pour	essuagi nenje		

Present or Future Tense   *Imperative Mood*

Infinitive of **to milk** = $\begin{cases}\text{nebegul (singular)}\\\text{negebegngul (plural)}\end{cases}$

I milk or will milk	aleb nanu		
Thou milkest or wilt milk	eleb iye	Milk thou	talebo
He she or it milks or will milk	keleb nenye		
We milk or will milk	keleb iog		
You milk or will milk	elebeleb ndai	Milk ye	endaleb
They milk or will milk	keleb nenje		

Infinitive of **to lie** = $\begin{cases}\text{nailejesho (singular)}\\\text{negilajishu (plural)}\end{cases}$

I lie or will lie	eaidelejare		
Thou liest or wilt lie	eardiyelejare	Lie thou	elejesho
He she or it lies or will lie	eardenenyelejaro		
We lie or will lie	keaidiog elejare		
You lie or will lie	eaidindai elejare	Lie ye	elejesho
They lie or will lie	keardinenje lejaie		

Infinitive of **to breed** = $\begin{cases}\text{neishu (singular)}\\\text{negishu (plural)}\end{cases}$

I breed or will breed	ainoda or itishu		
Thou breedest or wilt breed	ernortaiye	Breed thou	enorda
He she or it breeds or will breed	kernoda nenye		
We breed or will breed	kernodassiog		
You breed or will breed	enorda ndai	Breed ye	enorda
They breed or will breed	kernoda nenje		

Infinitive of **to suck** = $\begin{cases}\text{nernag (singular)}\\\text{neginag (plural)}\end{cases}$

I suck or will suck	anāk		
Thou suckest or wilt suck	nag iye	Suck thou	tarnag
He she or it sucks or will suck	kernag nenye		
We suck or will suck	kernag issiog		
You suck or will suck	kernag ndai	Suck ye	endarnag
They suck or will suck	kernagenenje		

Present or Future Tense   Imperative Mood

Infinitive of **to sew** = {naribeshu (singular)
{negerebeshu (plural)

I sew or will sew	aribeshu nanu		
Thou sewest or wilt sew	aribeshu iye	Sew thou	tereba
He she or it sews or will sew	aribeshu nenje		
We sew or will sew	keribishiog		
You sew or will sew	eieberb ndai	Sew ye	enderibishu
They sew or will sew	eribishu nenje		

Infinitive of **to throw** = {nananga (singular)
{neginana (plural)

I throw or will throw	erananga iyi		
Thou throwest or wilt throw	tanganaiye	Throw thou	tanganai
He she or it throws or will throw	keianganaiyi nenje		
We throw or will throw	keianganaitissiog		
You throw or will throw	eianganait ndai	Throw ye	endananga
They throw or will throw	eranganaiti nenje		

Irregular Verbs.

Infinitive of **to say** = {nēro (singular)
{negero (plural)

I say or will say	etejo nanu		
Thou sayest or wilt say	nananorojo	Say thou	toojo
He she or it says or will say	erioijo		
We say or will say	kitaijai iog		
You say or will say	endai nariijo	Say ye	endojo
They say or will say	anaketijo		

Infinitive of **to ask** = {negiligwena (singular)
{negingiligwan (plural)

I ask or will ask	aigiligweno		
Thou askest or wilt ask	ingiligweanaiye	Ask thou	giligwena
He she or it asks or will ask	egiligwana		
We ask or will ask	kigiligwñenutwa		
You ask or will ask	kigiligwñeana ndai	Ask ye	engiligwena
They ask or will ask	anaingiligwñena		

Present or Future Tense　　　　　　　*Imperative Mood*

Infinitive of **to die** $=\begin{cases}\text{naii or ää (singular)}\\ \text{eyogee (plural)}\end{cases}$

I die or shall die	aia nanu		
Thou diest or wilt die	ēeɲi	Die thou	etua
He she or it dies or will die	kee nenye		
We die or shall die	ekee iog		
You die or will die	kie ndai	Die ye	etua
They die or will die	ketwada ninji		

Infinitive of **to fight** $=\begin{cases}\text{naiirishu or naarr (singular)}\\ \text{negierishu (plural)}\end{cases}$

I fight or will fight	ataaia		
Thou fightest or wilt fight	etaarii	Fight thou	taaia
He she or it fights or will fight	aataosho		
We fight or will fight	kitioshosidu		
You fight or will fight	etaara ndai	Fight ye	endaiaada
They fight or will fight	etaaiade nenje		

Verbs of Negation

I can	aidim nanu
Thou canst	endem iye
He she or it can	kaidem nenye
We can	keendem iog
You can	kedem ndai
They can	kedem nenje

I cannot	maidim
Thou canst not	meedem
He she or it cannot	maidem nenye
We cannot	meedem iog
You cannot	meedem ndai
They cannot	meedem nenje

Present or Future Tense   *Imperative Mood*

I do not or shall not like	manyorr		
Thou dost not or wilt not like	minyorr		
He she or it does not or will not like	menyori ninyi		
We do not or will not like	mekinyoiiiyog		
You do not or will not like	menyorr ndai		
They do not or will not like	menyorr ninji		
I do not or will not wait	maanyo		
Thou dost not or wilt not wait	main iye	Wait not	mianyo
He she or it does not or will not wait	maanyo nenye		
We do not or will not wait	mitianyi yoog		
You do not or will not wait	mitianyo ndai	Wait ye not	emianyo
They do not or will not wait	miyu nenje nian-yuio		
I do not or will not eat	etu nananya		
Thou dost not or wilt not eat	etu nwananya	Eat not	emenyenda
He she or it does not or will not eat	etu nenjenye		
We do not or will not eat	etu siog enye		
You do not or will not eat	anaketu nanya	Eat ye not	emenya
They do not or will not eat	ketu nenjene		
I do not or will not drink	etu nanawok		
Thou dost not or wilt not drink	ketuyiwok	Drink not	emiog
He she or it does not or will not drink	ketwog nenye		
We do not or will not drink	etossiog iog		
You do not or will not drink	ketundai woki-woko	Drink ye not	emiog
They do not or will not drink	ketuog nenje		

Present or Future Tense		*Imperative Mood*
I do not or will not want	maıyu	
Thou dost not oı wilt not want	mıyu	
He she oı ıt does not or will not want	meyu nenye	
We do not or will not want	meyu iog	
You do not oı will not want	meyu ndaı	
They do not or will not want	meaw nenje	

PHRASES.

Phrases of Negation.

I do not know	maiulu
I do not understand	etunanwaiing or etoaning
I do not want	maiu
I will not go	etwaolo
I will not diink	etwaowok
I will not retuin	marrinyinyi or etwaininyi
I will not make	etu nainorebei
I do not want to go	maiyu nanunalo
I have not seen anything	etwa adoldogi
I do not like that man	maiu eireltungani
Not good	me sidai
Not bad	mer toiono
No water	mer ngare
No food	mer nda
Not large	me kitok
He will not biing	eteau
You will not heai	eturenyi
We will not come	etiyu kibonu
They will not know	maiulo ninji
He will not say	etweja nenye
We will not drink	etu kiog
You aie not old	meiagitok
You have not seen anything	etuiye edoldogi
He has not seen me	etwadol nenye
We have not seen anyone	etiyo kidologonanyi
They have not seen me	etwadol ninji
We do not want to go	mikiieyu nigibu
They do not want to fight	miyau niarara
Do not biing food	meiaw nda
Do not biing water	meiaw ngaie
We will not carry	etuyōgei
Not this man, the other one	meieltungani, legai

Phrases of Interrogation

What is your name?	kejinai ngairana inu?
What is the time?	kabai ngolong? (lit. where is the sun?)
What are you doing?	ainyo endobei?
What is this?	ainyena?
What do you want?	ainyoiyu?
What medicine do you want?	ainyo oldyani hū?
What news or what?	ainyo?
Why are you waiting?	ainyo erjano?
Where are you going?	kajilu oi ajilo?
Where is your sister?	koie anganashe ingu?
Where is the child?	kore ngeiai?
Where do you come from?	kajingwaia?
Where is my knife?	koie olalim elai?
Why sleep?	ainyo beioia oi oberora?
Why eat?	ainyo begenoss?
Why drink?	ainyo beiok?
Why good?	ainyo basidai?
Why cry?	ainyo beenjirr?
Why dance?	ainyo begeiran?
Why come?	ainyo belotu?
Why go?	ainyo belo?
Why I?	ainyo bananu?
Why he?	ainyo banenye?
Why meat?	ainyo bangirii?
What do you want to say?	ainyo iyu nēro?
Does he want to bring his child here?	eyu nerigu ngerai nyenne?
Do they want to return?	keyu nenje nerrinyu?
Do you want to return?	iyu iye neiiinyu?
Do they want to ask for anything?	kuyu nenje ngiligwena toki?
Does he want to see me?	eyu nenye nadol?
Do you want to see me?	iyu nadol iye?
Will you eat?	mossaiiye?

Phrases to illustrate the Infinitive Mood.

I want to go	aiyu nanu nalo
Do you want to come?	iyu nilotu?
Do you want to go?	iyu nilu?
They want to build a boma	keyu neegair engang
He does not want to wait	meyu nuanyorr
I want to bathe	aiyu naisoja
I want to wake early	aiyu naiogi ainyorodo
I want to drink	aiyu nawog
I want to sleep	aiyu nanora
We want to bathe	iyu negasoja
I want to boil water	aiyu naitokitok ngaie
Do they want to eat?	kiyu nenya?
We want to drink	iyu ngiog
I do not want to eat	maiyu nanya
We want to say	kiyu negero
I want to sit down	aiyu naidon
I want to look	aiyu nengora
Does he want to drink?	keyu nawok?
I want to hear	aiyu nanu nani
We want to fight	kiyu ngigerishu
I want to know	aiyu nanu naiulu
To eat now	nanya taada
I want to finish the work	aiyu naideba ingias
I want to call the child	aiyu naibot ngerai
He wants to climb the tree	eyu negent oldiani
We want to buy cows	kiyu neginyawng ngishu
He wants to cook the food	eyu neyeir nda
They want to clean the boma	keyu nooi engang
They want to wait	keyu niñnyu
We want to take away the things	kiyu iog naidaw ndogitin
You want to dance	iyu nengoiran
We want to dance	kiyu negigorran
We want to heal	kiyu negining
I want to fight	aiyu naari
We want to sing	kiyu negerran
They want to sit down	keyu nenje netornyi

We want to look	kiyu negongoii
They want to come	keyu nenye nebon
He wants to ask	eyu negiligwan
We want to bring food	kiyu iog negiaw nda
I want to come	aiyu nalotu
We want to know	kiyu iog negiolog
We want to give	kiyu negenjog
I want to carry my gun	aiyu nanab enduil lai
They want to finish work	keyu nedebai ngias
I want to laugh	aiyu nakweni
They want to call	keyu nenje nĕebot
I want to die	aiyu naii
He wants to buy goats	eyu nenyong ndari
We want to cook the food	kiyu negiyen nda
I want to clean the house	aiyu naoir ngaji
I want to wait	aiyu naanyo
They want to break stones	keyu neeidan ossoito
I want to dig a garden	aiyu nairem ngurruma·
I want to build a house	aiyu nanu nairaw ngaji
He is going to beg	eyu nenye niomon
We want to put	kiyu negiragi
We want to spit	kiyu neginoitagi
We want to steal meat	kiyu negibirro ngirri
I want to refuse	aiyu ān
They want to refuse	keyu nenje nian
You want to run away	eyu nilwaiyer
We want to run away	kiyu negilwaiyei
I want to pour out water	aiyu nabeg ngare
We want to pour out water	kiyu negibeg ngare
He wants to milk the cows	eyu nebegul ngishu
They want to milk the cows	keyu negibegngul ngishu
He is going to hunt	eyu nengorishu
We want to hunt	kiyu iog negingorishu
I want to forget	aiyu nariginu
I want to sew	aiyu naribeshu
We want to sew	kiyu negerebeshu
She is going to breed	eyu neishu

Phrases in the First Person Singular.

I am cold	aning ingijāpi
I am hot	airogua nalin
I am hungry	aralameu
I am ill	aemwi
I am angry	ābe
I am going to the coast	alogisho kishwanni
I am making medicine	aisholdyani
I am very ill	aemwi ossupati
I am going yonder	aloiiti
I am well	aishwosa nanu
I am old	nanu kitok
I drink milk	awokule
I am good	ara supatt
I am afraid	awuri
I want water	aiyu ngare
I want medicine	aiyu oldyani
I have called the man	aideba aihōdo eltungani
I have a stomach-ache	aia ngoshogi
I will eat	anyanda
I will bring food now	aiaw taada nda
I will shoot	alaara
I have made medicine	aideba endobera oldyani
I will give you food	aiisho nanu nda
I hear a noise	atoringu oibilebelebebe
I will kill the cow	aiyeng ngiting
I will return	arrinyinyi
I have slept long	airora osupati
I want more water	aiyu aiare
I want more milk	aiyu gulele
I want more meat	aiyu gulēgirri

Phrases to illustrate the Possessive

I have a spear	aad eiemet
I have a child	aadang ngerai
I have a father *	aada baba

* The words father (*baba*) and mother (*yeyu*) in Masai are only used by children with reference to their own parents it is considered both unlucky and insulting to address the parents of others in these terms. When refer-ring to the parents of other people, the terms *minyi* or *menye* are used for father, and *nautnnay, naotonay, nutun* or *notorn* for mother

I have a mother*	aara nanu yeyu
You (sing) have a shield	eeta elongo
You (sing) have a child	ere ngerai
You (sing) have a father*	errai eminyi
You (sing) have a mother*	errai ngutungy
He has a sword	eerda nenye olalim
He has a child	err ngerai iye
He has a father*	eira menye
We have spears	ker eiremeta
We have no children	miker ngera
We have a father	kerrai iloababa
You (pl.) have swords	erra ndai lalima
You (pl) have children	eria ndai ngera
You (pl) have a father*	eira ndai minyi
They have spears	erra nenj eriemeta
They have no children	meira nenje ngera
They have a father*	erra menye
My child	ngeraie
My children	ngeraiini
My hand	ngaiinai
My bottle	oldulelai
My bag	orbenelai
My father	babalai
My mother	yeyulai
Your (sing.) father*	minyeli
Your (sing) mother*	ngutungvi
Your (sing.) child	ngerainno
Your (sing) spear	erremetino
His father*	minyiye
His mother*	ngotongiye
His gun	endiulenye
His sister	nganashenye
Our father	baba elang
Our mother	yeyoŏg
Our children	ngerang
Our cows	ngishuung
Our boma	engangang
Your (pl) father*	minyi linyi
Your (pl.) mother*	nutun inyi
Your (pl) dog	orldia linyi

Your (pl.) skins	oljoni linyı
Their mother*	notornenye
Their house	engajenye
Their medicine	oljanıenye
Their father*	mınyenye or menye

.

Phrases to illustrate the Imperative.

Pour out a little more water	tebeg ngıtı aıare
Bring drinking water	ıaw ngarc nau
Make a fire	ınua ngıma
Boil the water	endogodogı ngare
Call the man	embooto eltungani
Be quiet	endegerrara
Go away	ınno
Come here	woo enne
Bring food	ıaw nda
Put it outside	eragiiı bo
Bring hot water	iaw ngare naırogua
Look or come here	ēro
Get out of the way	ewanga oı engıriıu
Go with me	maabe ooje
Make medicine	endobera oldjanı
Wait for me	taınyogı
Take away the food	todomu nda
Tell the woman to come here	tıagı engıtok oo enne
Tell me the truth	tollugiogı supatı
Wake me early	nenyegı taadagenıa
Open the door	tobollo kutugajı
Shut the door	ıngieno kutugajı
Give me water	enjoogı ngaıe
Come back soon	ınoberinınyı
Do not return	merrınyinyı
Bring more food	ıaw ıaıda oı eatataı
Take the things away	endaw ndogıtin
Bring more men	torrigu kelogaıtungana
Bring more children	torrıgu gulegera
Bring more cows	teıııaw gulegıshu

~ See footnote, page 35.

Bring more cold water	iaw aiaie naiiobi
Bring more chairs	iaw orrigaiishi
Bring more bottles	iaw illigaidulet
Give me milk	enjoogi nanugule
Give me meat	enjoōg nguri
Give me food	enjoogi nda
Give me more milk	enjoogi guhele
Give me more meat	enjoogi gulēgirii

Phrases.

A big boy	sabuk orlaion
A big child	ngerai boidori
A big woman	engitok sabuk
The boys are bad	egogong elaiyoik
The men are good	supati koilungana
The lions are fierce	inossisho logwaru
A long house	ēido ngāiiji
A black goat	ndaii naiok
Many black goats	kumuk ndaii nāiok
A red cow	ngitmg ainyuki
Many red cows	ngishu nyainyuki kumuk
A stupid woman	ershall ngoriion
Stupid women	ershall kenangoirriok
A bad man	egogo eltuugani
Bad men	egogo oiiltuugana
A strong horse	ebē imbaiida
Strong horses	ebē mbaiidan
The child has gone	eshomo ngerai
The children have gone	eshomo ngeia
The man has come	ewar eltungani
The men have come	ietu eldongana
A big man	eltungani sabuk
Two big men	sabuki oiildongana ari
Four good children	supati konengeia uugwun
Five large cows	sabuki ngishu miet
Three good women	sidai engitua ooni
A big donkey	sabuk issigerria
Big donkeys	sabuki ollissirigon
How much?	kaija?

To give gratis	aishu apeshu
I say	iya
To express thanks	kitaritu
To make a noise	obilebelēbebe or elebeleb
Are you ill?	imwe?
How many men are there here?	kaija eltungana enne?
The rain is near	eteana ngai
You are dirty	eata olaireriu
How many eggs are there here?	kaija mossori enne?
Are you tired?	eji enawri
It will rain in the night	ewar ngai kawarie
They are all going	eshomo bōōgi
This smells bad	ellele
The wind is strong	aikitok ollimwa
The wind is not strong	mekitok ollimwa
The clothes are wet	aishai ngelaui
There are forty zebras	eti loidugoi aiitam
I have seen thirty-one congoni	airadu origorigori ossom oobo
I have seen a hundred cows	airadua ngishu ip
There are fifteen goats here	eti enne ndari tomonoimiet
You have told a lie	edegwela elejere
The journey is long	kitok ennasapari
You have stolen my goats	etuburoi ndairai
You go to-day	ilo taada
You have gone	edeba shomo
In a little while	eirongonongon oi kiti kweji
We want to drink	kiju iog nkiog
You have seen ten children	eitadua ngera tomon
We have seen many children	eriadua ngera kumuk
More rain is coming	ewai aii
Under the trees	aboii oljani
They have made a big war	etobeia engitok weji
They are having a big dance	eti ngigoian edeweji
We will go for a walk	kibeba aileleta
He is coming	nyelolutu
You and I will go out	kibwa ellela alileta
The dog and cat are friends	enoyi oldia mbarrie
You and I	nanoiye
The dog and cat	oildia embairie
The man and woman	eltungana engitok
The sheep and goats	ngerr engini
The cows and goats	ngishu oidari
You and he	nenyoive

You are angry	egogo ıye
He is old	atakıtok
We are afraid	kıewre
You (pl.) are foolısh	emadada ndaı
He is bad	serrseri
You (sıng.) are good	eraıye supatt
He ıs good	sıdaı nenye
He is hungry	erda lameǔ
You (sıng.) are hungry	etala meǔ
We are good	kera sidan
We are old	kera dasat
We are hungry	kera lameǔ
They are good	sıdanenje
They are old	morruanenje
They are afraıd	arraıuıe

SALUTATIONS.

Salutation to a woman (literally "laugh")	tagwenia
„ „ „ (plural)	tagwenia bōōgi
Reply	īgo
To a man	soboi
Reply	eber
On shaking hands	nassak

Song the children sing for rain.

Siumbi aielisiumbi ngai kijaiga eo!
God we sing, God rain we pray thee oh!

Medicine Song

Aamon yi ngai, aamon m'Batian.
We pray God, we pray Batian

Song sung by the warriors when going to fight Sendeyo.

Sendeyo manoloimoti tendeboi eiiakenja bonik oldash iriemeta.

Sendeyo has done evil, we were friends once but now we go to fight him
with our spears, the big ones in front the small behind.

Hunters	Orrmāssani	Singular of Masai
	elmāsai	Plural of Masai
	{ olldōriobon	Singular
	{ dōriobo	Plural
Iron workers	{ oiigunoni	Singular
	{ elgunonu	Plural

Kenia (mt.)	oldonyo gēri (the striped mountain)
Kilima Njaro (mt)	oldonyo eboir (the white mountain)
Suswa (mt.)	oldonyo kenyuki (the red mountain)
Nairobi (river)	Cold (the river comes from the forest and is very cold as it emerges into the open)
Ngongo bagas (river)	(the eye of the Spring)
Eldonyo sabuk (mt)	(the big mountain)
Gwasso kidong (river)	the river of the ollokidong trees (the wood of these trees is used for making quivers)
Enaibasha (lake)	the great water or sea

Curses

Djeri terrā	A curse against the man addressed
Njeitēirda	Against the man addressed
Mining jangayenda	Against a man and his father
Kurigūmini	A curse on the father saying the person cursed is a bastard
Injerau	This curse is supposed to cause the death of a brother or sister
Tadui munigihdoigi	This curse is supposed to cause the person addressed to die
Injerai kordai	A child's curse
Munjirria nigiruk	A child's curse
Mbussa bwaara	Fool
Mbaria	This is accompanied by spitting and is the equivalent of damn

VOCABULARY

A

abdomen (lower)	enganoiri
acacia (wild)	osseneyer
across (water)	talanga
adjoining	ertasha
adjudge* (v. Imp)	tudungu oiiori (literally, to cut the noise or difficulty)
adulteress	kiborrong
afiaid	awure gurede
afternoon	engeberada ngolong
afterwards	tengai, ade
again	enagi
ahead	nologonya
alive	biotu
all	boogi
all of us	io boogin
allow (v. Imp)	aishoilu
all right	aiya
aloe	oldoboi
alone	nanu wake (literally, I alone)
also	oshiagi
altei (v Imp)	imenejengo
always	engolong eboogi (literally, all days or suns)
angry	abe, ebi
ankle	olloregogoiyu pl. loirigegiru
anklets (of skin)	emonge pl mmongen
answer (v Imp.)	tedema
ant (laige black)	olloisuisui

* All the verbs have been given in the Imperative, as well as many in the Infinitive mood, since it is possible, before mastering the conjugations, to make oneself undeistood in Masai by using the Imperative Mood only It is, theiefore, impoitant that the Imperatives should be learnt first.

ant (small black)	engalāū
ant (red, siafu)	emuyu pl muyu
ant (white)	orrırı pl. ıııaı
antelope	engoih pl. engōīlın
anything	toki
apace	engueriaia
arm (the whole)	ngaına pl ngaıeg
aım (foıe)	endagūle pl endagūlın
aım (uppeı)	orbeıangash pl elbeıangashi
aımpıt	ngıtīgıtı pl ngıtigıt (lıteıally, tıckle)
arrıve (v. Imp.)	keıabaaıdı
arrow	embaı pl. embā
ashes	nguıruwun pl nguriuwun
ask (v. Imp.)	engīlıgwena, ngıligwena (Infin.)
at once	taada
awake (v. Imp.)	ınyo
axe	endōlu pl. endōluĕr

B

baboon	olldōlal pl olldolalli
back	engorııong pl. engōırıong
back (small of)	ollōıo pl. olloroom
bad	egogong (anımate objects)
bad	torono (ınanımate objects)
bag	oııbenı pl eлebenı
banana	elmaısuıı pl. olmaısuri
baobab tree	ollıııseıa
baıb (of aırow)	essebıl pl essebıllı
baık (v. Imp.)	tabua
bark (of tree)	engabobook pl. engabobook
barrenness	olupı mer engeıa
basket*	engıondo (kıkuyu) pl. engıondonı
bastard	engeıaı orlatolac (lıteıallყ, child of dirt)
bathe (v. Imp)	aısojaı $\begin{cases} \text{naısoja (sıng.)} \\ \text{negasoja (pl)} \end{cases}$ Infin
beads	mussıtanı or osaın pl. essaın
beak	olloroıom pl. olloıorom
beard	oırımunyı pl. oırımunyı

* The Masaı have no woıd foı basket, and make use of the Kekuyu woıd.

because	aiinyo
bed	eriuat pl eriuati
bee	oltoroki pl lodorok
beer (native)	enjoii
beetle	oriomwila pl elmwiela
beg (v. Imp.)	toomonu, namon (Infin.)
beggar	orlāmonon pl lāmonok
belch	olljerādi
bell (small)	enduela pl. endwalan
bell (cow)	engorrogoir pl engorrogorru /
bell (warrior's)	oldwalan pl eldwalan
bellows	engune pl. engunēi
belt	ingitadi pl. inkitadin
bend (v Imp)	torrigu $\begin{Bmatrix} \text{neirin (sing)} \\ \text{negirriu (pl)} \end{Bmatrix}$ Infin
better	ishigo, ingiwa
between	porrloss
bird	ndandigi pl. ndandig
birds (small)	engelloguny
bite (v Imp)	toonyo, erionyo, nawon (Infin.)
bitter	edua
black	erok
bladder (animal)	origulet pl orrgulet
blade (of knife)	essibir orlalim
blade (of spear)	essibirr
blaze (v.)	orlangal
blind person	mordon pl elmodon
blood	assarge
blow nose (v.)	enduymo guluk
blow (v Imp.)	tokodar, neenok (Infin)
blue	mbusth ollonyori
boat	etawalānget
body	oesesi pl essessin
bog	earsurr pl earsuri
boil (v Imp)	endogidogi or etokitok, naitokitok (Infin)
boma (zariba)	'engang pl engangiti
bone	olontu pl. lonk
boot	enamoki pl namoka
border	erreshata
bore (v. Imp.)	tariemo
born (v.)	nitoushi (Infin)
both	bogiran (literally, all two)
bottle	oldulet pl olduleta

M. G.   4

bow	ngaw pl ngaṇ
boy	oɩlaɩyon pl. laɩyok
boy (little)	laɩyōnɩgɩtɩ
bracelet	oɩgatñ pl elkataɩɩ
brain	ollālogonɩa or ollaɩbrinyi pl. ollaɩbrɩnyɩnyɩ
branch	eṇgossela pl. enlenōssel
bɩeak (v. Imp)	tegēlla, negɩl (Inﬁn)
breast	orrɩgena pl. ellgɩē
breed (v Imp.)	eɩɩoɩshɩ, neɩshu (Infin.)
bridge	orlanget pl. langerta
bɩɩng (v. Imp.)	ɩaw, ncgɩaw (Infin.)
bɩɩng forth (about to)	eṇdua
broad	dabash
brooni	alāraw pl. alārawon
brother	ollalashe pl. ollalashera
brother-in-law	olabadaṇɩ pl elabatak
buffalo	alāɩu pl. elāroɩɩ
build (v. Imp)	engarɩa or desherder, naɩraw (Inﬁn)
bull	orlōīngoṇɩ pl. oɩlaɩngok
buɩn (v. Iɩnp)	eēka
burr	endeɩɩobenyi
bury (v. Imp.)	toɩnoga
bush buck	ollbua
bustard (gɩeat)	kūgogēlɩ
bustard (lesseɩ)	orɩgēlababa pl. ellgeɩɩalababa
but	kakɩ
butter	engorɩno pl engoɩɩn
butterfly	ossamburubuɩ pl sambuɩuburu
buttocks	ollduḷɩ, ollgoɩom
buy (v Imp.)	enyāngu {nenyong (sing.)} Inﬁn {ɩɩegɩnawng (pl.)}
by myself	naṇu waki or wagi
by thyself	ɩyagɩ
by himself	ninyagɩ
by ourselves	ɩogagɩ
by youɩselves	ndaɩagɩ
by themselves	enɩnjagɩ

C

calf	olashɩ pl olasho
calf (of leg)	olldɩɩm
call (v Imp.)	emhōotu or emborru, naibot (Inﬁn)

camel	ndamess pl. ndarmessı ngaiurı
cap	engaıı auda pl. engārranda
captain	ollaıgwanan pl. laıgwanak
carross	engela nderı (litcıally, clothes of sheep)
caıry (v. Imp.)	tanabo. nanab (Infin.)
caı tridges	ossout lendıul (lıterally, stones of the gun)
castrate (v Imp)	egellema
cat	erongo oı mbāṛıe pl mbaıria
catch (v. Imp)	emboonga. $\begin{cases} \text{nebong (sıng)} \\ \text{negıbong (pl.)} \end{cases}$ Infin.
caterpillar	ollogurıto pl. olloguı rt
cat tııbe	logwāıu pl logwāıak
cause	endıaragi
centipede	ossambela pl ossambelali
central	enadoagada
chain	ollbīsıaı pl ıllbıssıa
chaıns (ın eaıs)	emōnaı pl emōna
chaıns (for brass eaıı ıngs)	illgoıēda
chaır	olōııka pl. lorrigaishi
chameleon	nottoıı angı pl. nottoıı angı
cheek	endagola pl. endagol
chest	orgoo, oıgon pl elgoon
chest (mıddle)	olludua
chew (tobacco)	enyalo orı gumbaw
chew (the cud)	enyang amura
chicken	elūgungu pl elugunguni
chıef	oı lebon pl. oıloıbonı
chıld	ngeıāī pl ngerā
chın	ollomoon oı orboōn
chirp (v Imp)	eoııtu
choose (v Imp.)	kaıyuatagona
cırcle	eboıogoran
cırcumcıse (v Imp.)	ermoırata
claws	oloısodo pl loisoıdok
clay	esseı angap
clean	čboıı
clean (v. Imp)	essoja, naorı (Infin)
clematıs (wıld)	engoıı ōgi
clever	ebi or ertangainyel
clımb (v. Imp)	tagedo, negıd (Infin)
cloth	engelā pl. engelanı
cloth (waıııoı's waı)	enanga
clothes	engelanı

4—2

cloud	engarrambuɪ pl. engarrambo
coast	enaɪbasha (lɪterally, the gɪeat sea)
cold	ngɪjūbɪ or eɪobi
cold (in head)	ebɪssēnga
collar	emāīraɪ pl mmālɪta
colobus monkey	orrgoɪroɪ pl ellgoɪroien
colouɪ	serret
come (v. Imp.)	ōōtuōō oɪ wōō, nalolu or nebo (Infin)
come back (ⅴ Imp.)	toɪrɪmɪnyɪ oɪ torɪɪnyo
conceal (v. Imp.)	ɛssudōiɪ
conceive	eɪnoda oɪ erreɪngu ngerai
conquer (v. Imp)	etuɪrua
cook (v. Imp.)	tɪaɪɪa $\begin{cases} \text{neyeɪ r (sɪng.)} \\ \text{negɪycrr (pl)} \end{cases}$ Infin
cookɪng vessel	emoti pl motiu
copulate (v.)	nenjoōgɪ ngumɪɪ (Infin.)
coɪd	engeenda pl engeenda
cotton	embɪtu pl. embɪt
cough	engeɪɪoget
count (v. Imp.)	engc̄ena
country	ngop pl. ngop
coveɪ (ⅴ Imp.)	tebessenga
cow	ngetēhbong, ngɪtɪng (head oɪ cattle) pl ngɪshu
cow-killing house	ollobul pl ellbulɪ
coward	gurede pl guredɪ
cowry	ossegeraɪ pl essegera
crab	essuɪusuɪɪ
crawl (a man)	eerbeɪebaɪɪɪ
creep (an anɪmal)	essberbaɪrɪ
crested crane	enaitolɪ pl. enaɪtolia
crɪcket	surūsurī
crocodɪle	oɪɪgenōss pl ergenossin
crow (whɪte necked)	orgorrok pl elgūɪruki
crow (v. Imp)	eoɪɪtu
crush (v. Imp.)	eɪronⅴa
cry (ⅴ Imp)	ɪsheeɪa oɪ injeeɪa neenjerr (Infin)
cup (dɪɪnkɪɪg vessel)	orɪbugurɪɪ
cuɪe	esshɪvo
custom	supatt (lɪterally, what is good)
cut (v. Imp.)	tudungɪɪ $\begin{cases} \text{nadung (sɪng.)} \\ \text{negɪdung (pl.)} \end{cases}$ Infin.

D

dance	ingiguian pl maiguiana
dance (v.)	{nengorian (sing.)} {negigorran (pl.)} Infin.
dark	enaimen
dawn	etawanga oi engagenia
day	ngolong pl ngolong
day after to-moirow	ngaiolong
daylight	dāma
dead body	etuer
deat	etwani
dear (price)	eigol
deep	orrmoti
deny (v. Imp.)	enjangāir
dew	engoileli
diairhoea	equet ngoshogi (literally, running away of the stomach)
die-die	essūni pl essūni
die (v. Imp)	etua. naii (Infin.)
difficult	eigol
dig (v Imp)	tuduru
dint	olloieiiyu or oilatolac
dirty	essūd
disembowel (v. Imp.)	tadanya ngoshogi
divide (v. Imp.)	endoir
dog	orldia pl. eldiain
donkey (female)	ossigiriia pl. issirigŏn
donkey (male)	olāinwe pl ellamweishi
dooi	kutugaiji pl. engutuengaij k
do you heai	ēji oi etoningu
diaw (water) (v.)	ndogua ngare (Infin.)
dieam	aideiidet
diink (v. Imp)	tooko, niog oi nawok (Infin.)
drive away (v Imp.)	temerra
dium	ossingoilu pl ossingoilu
drunk (to be)	etemeiie
duck	emotoiioki pl. emotoiok
dumb	eiebogotok
dung (cow's)	emodue pl modiok
dust	endeiit
dust storm	ollimwa
duyker (antelope)	mpaiuāss pl mpainass

E

eagle	ormotonyingeiu pl. oimotonyingeioi
eai	engiok pl ingīā
ear (animal's)	menĕss
eai (lobe)	essegeiiua
ear (top edge)	oirgedebet
ear (hole in lobe)	essĕgeirua
early	taadagenia or peiko
early (veiy)	taiku
earring	essurutie pl. essorudia
earwig	engolōpa
easy	endobeia nagititogi (literally, doing small things)
eat (v. Imp.)	inosa, nanya (Infin.)
egg	emossoiri pl emosorr
egret	enairlĕli
eight	issiet
eighteen	tomonoissiet
eight times	katitin issiet
eland	ossiiiwa pl issīiiiwai
elbow	ollaidolol pl. oiloidolloli
elder	elbaiyen kitok
elephant	eldonyioirosabuk pl eldanga sabuki oi elan-gaiina or oldome
elephant grass	ollgerrioni
eleven	tomononabu
end	ebaiyi
endure (v. Imp.)	tegeraiye meio
enemy	ormangatinda pl elmaigati
entrails	embulati
equal	errisui
Europe	geshuaini
every	bōōgi
everything	edogiding bōōgi
evil eye	egurrtoōng oi possongu
exchange	mataoilage
eye	ngongo pl. ngonyek
eyebiows } eyelashes }	elbabit ngongo (hteially, the hairs of the eies)
eyelid (upper)	shomata ngong (the roof of the eie)
eyelid (lowei)	aboii ngong (under the eye)
eye (pupil of)	nerok ngong (the black of the eye)
eye (white of)	eboii ngong (the white of the eie)

F

face	ngomom pl ngomom
faint	olloididua
fall (v. Imp.)	erabaiadi nebaiada (Infin)
fai	orelagua or elakwa
fast	tāssiogi
father	baba
father-in-law	bageii
father-in-law (who gives cows)	bageten
feather	ingobiiri pl. ngobirr
feed (cattle, v. Imp)	erieda
female	ngitok pl. ngituak
female (term of oppiobiium)	ngoiraiyon pl ngoirroiok
fifteen	tomon oimiet
fifty	orrnoin
fight (v. Imp.)	etaaia $\begin{cases} \text{naar (sing)} \\ \text{negigerishu (pl)} \end{cases}$ Infin.
fig-tree (wild)	olloboin
fill (v Imp)	eboiri
find (v Imp.)	erradua
finger	orkimojinu pl irrkimojik
finger (1st)	sagurishe
finger (2nd)	olgeiedi
finger (4th)	ingilinda
finish (v. Imp.)	edebi oi tabala, naideba (Infin.)
fii-cone	ollinoioi
fiie	ngima pl ngima
fiiewood	elgēg
fish	ossengeii pl essengerr
fish-bones	orgigui (lit. thoins)
fist	endololong ngaiina (the shut hand)
five	emiet
five times	kataimiet
flea	loisusu pl. loisusu
floui	engūiruma
flower	ndābogai pl ndaboga
fly	ellojonga pl. ellojonga
fly (v. Imp.)	eēda oi ebido, nebui (Infin)
fold (v Imp)	teena, neyen or ngened (Infin)
foliage	mbenck

follow (v. Imp.)	tossoja
food	ndā pl. ndaugi
fool	emwāda pl. emwāda
foot	ngaju pl ngaijek
forehead	ngomom pl. ngomom
forest	endim pl indimi
forget (v. Imp.)	adoiigin, ariginu (Infin)
forty	airtam
four	ungwun
fourteen	tomon ungwun
four times	kat ungwun
friend	oldyore pl. eldjoiduweta
frog	endua pl enduan
froth	olabara
frown	issot ngomom
fruit	eiangnaiyu oi olongaboili
full	epotā or ebotā
furnace	origoguet

G

game (alive)	ngwess pl. ngwessi
game (meat)	ingēiingu
game trap	orrgerenget
garden	ngurruma
gather (v. Imp.)	tadotu
gazelle (Grant's)	orrgwāiiagas pl oirgwāriagassi
gazelle (Thompson's)	engobeia pl. engoobeia
gentle	enana
get (v. Imp)	inodo oi anordo
get ahead	togiioii
get into	tejenagi
get out of the way	ingeriiu
ghost	essicati eltungani
giddy	amana elogonya
giraffe	oladōgaiagat pl eladoiugeraget
girl	nairo oi endoiyi pl ndito
girl (little)	nditogiti
give (v. Imp)	enjōōgi {nenjog (sing.)} {negenjog (pl)} Infin
give chase	etemeia
give trouble	ketelaniana

glad	eshēba
glitter	elio
gnaw (v Imp.)	tanyāala
go (v. Imp)	shomo, nalo (Infin.)
go after	etosoja
go away (from a place)	edora
go bad	errarrui
go round	tamanāī
go together	endoiobaia
goat	ndari pl ndāii
goat (castrated)	oirgiri pl. engineji
goat (female)	ingine pl ingineti
goat (female before bearing young)	essuben pl essubeni
goat (male)	orlōrio pl. orlorioi
god	ngai pl. ngai
good	sidai
good (very)	āīya
gourd	embuguri pl. embuguritu
gradually	aketi
grandparent	ngaguya
grass	engojeta pl. engojet
grasshopper	endargēeti pl endarigēet
gratis	peshu
grave	engumoto
graze (v Imp)	arda
great	sabuk
greedy	en̄lu
green	ainyoii
grey	mbustli oi gwarigoi
grey hairs	ebori elogonya (white head)
grief	ossomet
ground	ngop or enguluguk
grow (v. Imp)	etubulwa
growl	aiguriuguriu
guard	oriibi
guinea-fowl	origeiisuie pl elgeiiisurreni
gums	enyeiit
gums (at side)	eldagiligil
gun	endiul pl endioli
guts	mainyet

H

hair	olbabeta pl. elbabıt
half	ematua
hammer	orrgırrısıet
hand	ndap pl. ndapı
hand (palm of)	ndap ngaıına
hang (on wall, v. Imp.)	tolluwa
hasten (v. Imp.)	tassıogı guerdeı
hate (v. Imp.)	aıba
hawk	ollābebu pl ollābebu
haze	errogenıa
he	nenye
head	elogonya pl. elogōn
head-dress (lıon skin)	ollogwaru
head-dress (ostrıch featheıs)	engurraru pl enguıraıunı
hear (v Imp)	atorningu $\begin{cases} \text{nanı (sıng)} \\ \text{negınıng (pl.)} \end{cases}$ Infin
heart	ōldaw pl eldawaja
heavy	iıruıshı
hedgehog	enjōlıss
heel	endudunıu pl. eududun
heıfer	endāwu
heıd	olljogut pl. eljogutı
here	enne
hıccup	engioget
hıde (v. Imp)	essudon
hıll	olosho pl. oıloıshon
hippopotamus	ollōmagaw pl erımagawl
his	enenye
hole	engūmoto pl. engumōt
honey	enaıshu pl. enanshı
honey box	engidong pl ıngıdong
hongo	endau olmoırossı
hoof	oloısodok pl oloısōdok
hoın	emoworı pl. emowarrak
hornbıll	oırgımasāja pl. elgemasajanan
hoıse	mbaırda pl mbaırdan
house	ngajı pl ngajıjik
how many?	keıaja or kaıja
hump	cııok pl cııoga

hungry	olameı
hunt (v. Imp)	ngorrori $\begin{cases} \text{nengorıshu (sıng.)} \\ \text{negıngorıshu (pl)} \end{cases}$ Infin
husband (my)	elmōııualaı
hush	endegeıata
hyæna	olnojeıı pl. engorjın

I

I	nanu
ibıs	momēra
ıbis (black)	engalıte
ıdle	erʂhall
ıll	emwı
ımpala (antelope)	ndaıagwet oı ollolubu pl. ndaıagweti
ın	atua
infect	etasuıoıı
in fıont	nologonʝa
ınheııt	eʝūngoıe
ınsıde	etıaatwa
ınstead	inoitabaııdı
ııon	essegēngı
ıron-sand	senyāı

J

ʝackal	mbaıʝıe pl mbaıııa
ʝıgger*	ndudu (kiswahılı)
ʝouıney	enaıdoıa pl enaıdoıak
ʝump (v Imp)	olloııdı
ʝuıııper	ndaıagwa

K

keep (ʋ Iıııp.)	shomoıııbıe
kıdney	ellaııauguʝı pl. ellaııaugut
kıll (v. Imp)	teyanga. neyeng (Iııfiıı)

* The ʝıgger was ıntroduced among the Masaı by the Swahılıʂ, and the Masaı descııbℓ ıt by the kıswahılı word " insect

kiss   atongurtuda
kite   orrgillılı pl ıllgillılın
knee   engŏngo pl. engong
knee hollow   cndango pl endangon
kneel (v. Imp)   tegelāñgo
knife   olalım pl. olalema
knife (small)   engalimgıtı
knife-handle   enjeıdalalım
knob-kerry   orrguma pl. ellguman
knob-kerry (royal)   onguma lessegenggaı
knock (v Imp)   engōoro

know (v Imp.)   eeolo or iolu $\begin{cases} \text{naıulu (sing.)} \\ \text{negiolog (pl)} \end{cases}$ Infin

knuckles   errobāt ırrkımojık
kudu   emālo pl. mıggıbu
kudu (lesseı)   engımossorok

L

lame   ňgojēnı
language   orroē
large   sabuk
last   korom

laugh (v Imp)   atagwenıa, or engwenıa $\begin{cases} \text{nakwenı (sıng.)} \\ \text{negigwena (pl.)} \end{cases}$ Infin.

lazy   ershall
lean (v. Imp.)   toshomagı essendai
lean on (v Imp)   tanāba
leave (v. Imp)   tabala
leaves   ımeıın
left hand   kedıene
leg   ollŏıeshet pl loııeshetı
leopard   ologwaıugerı pl ologwaıakeıın
let go   tāla
lichen   naıēro
lid   essīotı
lie   ellejoıe
lift (v. Imp.)   todomu, oı elebı
light   ētegenıa (no mıst)
lightning   ewungeı ngaı

like (v. Imp)   aınyorı $\begin{cases} \text{naanya (sing)} \\ \text{negenyoıı (pl)} \end{cases}$ Infin

like this	aneena
line	orgenat
line (boundary)	erreshata ungwapı
lion	ōlonātrıng pl elnatungyu
lips	enjionengotok
liquid	elebeck
liver	emoinuar
lizard	olloirurı pl. ollanērı
load	olola pl. ololan
locust	olomādı pl. ellemāāt
long	ērdo
long ago	ōpa
look (v Imp)	engorāīi {naıngora (sing.)} {negongorr (pl)} Infın
loose	meenussıbaıı
lose (v. Imp)	emena
lungs	oııgıbıe pl ırıigıbıu

M

mad	ollaıdıdua
maggot	ıllgıuu
magic	orgoiyatık pl. elgoīyatıkı, oı orjanga
maize	ellibaiak
make (v Imp.)	endobeıa, nerobeıa (Iufın.)
make love	aıju
male	ōlē pl. elēwa
man	eldungamı pl. eldongana
man (old)	elmōıuua pl. lemoıuuak
many	kumuk
many times	nkatıtın kumuk
marabout stoık	enādogos pl. enādogossı
mark	oırborınoto pl ırıgonot
marriage	enango engıtok
marrow	endōlıt pl endōlo
marry (v. Imp)	eugabūdı, or endobera eugabudı
mash (v. Imp)	tegēlla
me	nanu
measure (v. Imp)	tedema
meat	ingēııngu, or engerıı
medicınal herb (purge)	oldīuugoın
medicıne	oldyauı

medicine man	ollibaıyon or oılaıbon
melt (v. Imp)	ılangalanga
mid-day	enaıbırıı ngolong
middle	engabe
milk	ngŭlē
milk (v Imp)	talebo, nebegul (Infin.)
mimosa (white)	lleırāıyı pl lērra
mimosa (yellow)	enjorrāīyi
miscaıııage	etaherwehı
mist	errogenia
money	engosholoı
mongoose	ollgoııoı, oı ollbelıss
monkey	engema pl. engemai, oı naıokotok
month	elaba pl. elabaitin
moon	elaba pl elabaıtın
moon (new)	emoelaba
moon (day betoıe full)	olgādet
moon (ṫull)	olloınyon
moon (day after full)	olloınynkı (ıed moon)
more	gulı or elang
mornıng	taadagenıa
mosquıto	engojonganȷe
motheı	yeyu pl. noıyeyu
mother-in-law	bagerr
mountaın	eldōınyo pl. eldoınyo or oldonȷo
moustache	oırımunyı pl oırımunyı
mouth	ngukuk, ngotuk pl. ngutuki
mud	eseııengap
muscle	ossēnı, or sınıgı
mushroom	labaı
mutılate (v Imp)	endaıuyı
my	enaı or elaı
myself	eıanāīı, enaben, olloben

N

naıls (fingeı)	loısōdok
naıls (bıass, etc)	olldedu
naked	meıengela (no clothes)
name	ngāııana pl. ngāııana
uarrow	rongāī

navel	ossoroiia
near	eteana
neck	emurrt pl emuirtu
neck, nape of	essangurigili
necklace	enoirini pl. enoirin
necklace (beads and long iion chains)	ollōmutu
necklace (beads and shoit iron chains)	ngāīshu
necklace (iion wire & chains)	essenga
needle	ollodedu pl illdidi
nest	ngaji udaridig (the house of the buds)
new	naijuk
night	kawarie
nine	nawdu
nineteen	tomon nawdo
nine times	katitin nawdo
nipples	enguiig oiiigena
no	menenye
noise	orrori
none	meti, or ĕtu
no one	mer eldongani (no man)
nose	ngumi pl. ngumeshin
nose bone	olloioiom
nostrils	ollgulu ngumi
not	meti, oi ĕtu
nothing	meetoki
now	taāda
numbei	engeena

O

obey (v Imp.)	nimining
of (belonging to)	or
often	ngatitin kumuk
oil	ēlara pl ēelā
old	endasat, moiiua (animate objects), msana (in- animate objects)
once	nabu
one	nabu
one hundied	ip
on top	shumata

open (v. Imp)	tobollo, nebol (Infin)
oiatoi	ellaigwanan
orchilla weed	nareio
oidure	ingiek
orphan	orgisshi pl. engogishin
ostrich	essidaie pl. sidan
other	elegai
oui	enāang
outside	boo
overflow	etabongori ngaie
oversleep	ēemuk
overturn	embëllegeiia
owe	nessili (Infin.)
owl	elmagero

P

pain	ēme, or emwi
paint	ossiie
paint (black)	ngngu pl ngūk
paint (red)	ossoiet lolongoi
paint (white)	enduröto
palaver	oirori
palm	oldiani
pant (v Imp)	engebangibang or ebangibang
papei	embalai
papyrus	ollaibolignia, or ollannutie
partridge	engūrrle pl engoirlen
pay (v. Imp)	talagi
penis	enjābu pl. injabok
people	eloshon
perhaps	aāsho
pick (flowers, v. Imp.)	tadoju
pick (up, v. Imp)	todomu
pig	olbitirr pl. elbitiriu
pigeon	endūriugulu pl endurrugulum
pigmy	engogi
pig-tail	oldaiga pl oldaiigan
pinch (v. Imp.)	ctumunu
pipe	olomoti pl. elmotio
point (v. Imp.)	toada

poison	assaiyet, or olniorridue
poison tree	ollmorrije
pools	ngare nairora (lit. the sleeping waters)
poor	oilālsinan
porcupine	waiaiai pl. iaiya
potato*	ngwashin (kikuyu)
pour (v. Imp.)	tebego {nabeg (sing.)} {negibeg (pl.)} Infin.
place	eweji
plague	oldigana
plain	enguseru pl. engussēro
plantain-eater (green)	engeiwa pl. engeiwan
please (v. Imp.)	enyorr
pleuro-pneumonia	orrgibie
plume (v. Imp.)	irroberringbirr
pray (v. Imp.)	tassai ngai. namon Infin. or āamon. namor Infin.
precipice	endigirr
pregnant	enduā, or enota ingitok
present	olērinoire
presently	ardi, or tengai
prick (v. Imp.)	kitarrimu
prisoner	atarugagi
property	endogiai
prostitute	eneweje, or dito
pull (v. Imp.)	tierai, niyetu (Infin.)
pull out (v. Imp.)	tebello
punishment	taāra
purgative medicine	oldyanyinyuki, einogotōn, or loodwar
push (v. Imp.)	mbaionia
put (v. Imp.)	eragi {nebi (sing.)} {negiragi (pl.)} Infin.
put off (clothes)	endao engilani
put on (v. Imp.)	enjobo
put out (v. Imp.)	endau, or taara
put out (light)	taā ngima
putrefy (v.)	endungna

* The Masai use the kikuyu word, as the potato is only known to them through Wakikuyu medium.

Q

quail	orgẽllemɪ pl ɪllgẽlem
quarrel	etaɪɪgeno
quarter	tobelassa
quickly	tassɪogi
quiver (foɪ arrows)	emōdɪen pl emōdɪena

R

rabbɪt	engīroɪu pl. engīɪoɪu
ɪaɪn	ngaɪ pl. ngaɪ
raɪnbow	etau ngolong engang (lɪt. the boma of the sun)
ɪaɪse (v. Imp)	toɪdomo
rape	essemaɪye
ɪat	nderom pl. ndēɪo
raw	eɪɪon
razor	orɪomōronya pl ellemororanyɪ
reach (v Imp)	tabaigya
ready	edebɪ
ɪed	enyukɪ
ɪefuse (v. Imp.)	eɪɪanya nɪaɪɪ (Iɪfin)
remaɪnder	etungaɪ
ɪeɪnember (v Imp)	eɪɪadamua
repeat (v)	ngongaɪ taada (Iɪfin)
ɪesɪɪ	endeɪɪbenɪɪ
ɪest	enenenyɪ
return (v Imp.)	toɪɪɪnyoɪ oɪ ɪnyaɪ $\begin{cases} \text{naɪrem (sɪng.)} \\ \text{nerɪɪnyu (pl.)} \end{cases}$ Infin.
rhɪnoceros	emwoɪn pl. emwoɪnyɪ
ɪhɪnoceros-bɪrd	labuak or orlarrɪaki pl. larrɪak
rɪb	ollarassɪ pl. laɪass
rɪght hand	ndadem
rɪnderpest	ollodua
ɪɪɪɪg	orɪgɪsoɪ pl eɪɪgẽsso
rɪngworɪn	engāmunyān
rɪpe	eworto
rɪver	ngwasso, or oɪɪgēɪu, pl. elgegyat
road	ngōītɪɪ pl. ngoɪoɪtroɪ

roan antelope	ollbuwa
roof	shumarrotu pl. shumārrotu
root	endāanai pl. endaana
rotten	etomoti, or erradanyi
round	ellgegesat
rub (v. Imp.)	toōju, etiitü
run (v. Imp.)	equet
run away (v. Imp.)	essdoi {nilwaiyer (sing.) / negil waiyer (pl.)} Infin.
rushes	ollgojcra

S

safe	esserian
salt	emanyan
sandals	namōka
sand-grouse	enderregogo pl. enderregogo
sap	emānoi
savages	elmangati
say (v. Imp.)	tolimu, or ātoju, Infinitive nēro or negero
scab	orrbolōti pl. illbolōt
scabbard	enjāīshorr pl. enjaishorri
scar	ingiborōī pl. ingiborn
scent	ungwāi
scold (v. Imp.)	endarigyu
secretary-bird	engugogele pl. engugogele
seduce (v. Imp.)	endoraii
see (v.)	nadol (Infinitive)
seeds	enganaiji
sell (v. Imp.)	amer, or teemera
sense	enganyet
set on fire (v. Imp.)	tābejo
seven	nābishana
seventeen	tomon nābishana
seven times	katitin nābishana
sew (v. Imp.)	tereba {naribeshu (sing.) / negerebeshu (pl.)} Infin.
shadow	oloiipi pl. elloiipi
shake (v. Imp.)	mbiribiru
shake hands	tangassargi
shave (v. Imp.)	tabarrno, or narrbanugi
sheep (a)	ngera

sheep (female)	ngēir pl. ngēria
sheep (female before lambing)	essuben pl essubeni
sheep (male)	orimerēgi pl imeiregeshi
shield	elōngo pl. elongoi
shiver (v. Imp.)	engeiegeia
shoot (v. Imp)	dangoio, oi dara
shoit	doiop
shoulder	orron pl. irroin, or olloilelai pl ollailela
show (v. Imp)	endadua
shiew-mouse	ndedngumi
shut (v Imp)	tnbuguru {naigen (sing.)} {nigingen (pl.)} Infin.
sick (to be)	tollobishi
side	eimatua pl ematuan
sigh	engeanget, oi eanga
sinew	ēngonn, or emorito
sing (v Imp)	ossungolu {neeran (sing)} {negerran (pl.)} Infin., tairanya
sink (v. Imp)	mengare
sister	nganashe pl. nganasheia
sit (v Imp)	tordona {nardon (sing)} {netornyi (pl.)} Infin.
six	elle
sixteen	tomon oille
six times	kata ille
sixty	ip
skin	oldonyi pl. elonītu
skin (v. Imp)	iangada
skull	emborroborr pl mboiioboiii
sky	shomata
sleep (v Imp.)	eraga or erora naiiora (Infin.)
slip (v Imp)	esbēidet
slowly	aketi
small	ngiti
small-pox	endēdiai
smell (v Imp)	angwaiye, oi engongu
smoke	embūiruer
snail	orrbigitt pl. illbigitu
snake	oloserai pl. ellāsuiia
sneeze	engāssini
snipe	ollairie ngare
snore (v. Imp)	erongoiong
snow	endūroto

snuff	engisogi
snuff-box	orrgidong pl irigidong
sob	essogussu
soft	eruana
soon	eronongoii, oi engoir
sore	engerondo pl engerondoni
sore eye plant	alangungye
sort	enyaiyu
soup	umõiioiri
spaik	eldīclı pl edīṛ́l
speak (v Imp)	atoju, eioio
spear	eremet pl. iiiimeti
spear (end)	ollongoiat
speech	engigwani
spill (v Imp)	mbugoi, or endoiai
spine	ollorugot lenguiiiong
spit (v. Imp)	tornodoi {nenordargi (sing)} {neginoitaigi (pl)} Infin.
spittle	endaishala, oi engamolae
splinters	orgebeirati pl. elgeberiat
split (v. Imp)	tobolossa
spring (of water)	mbagas
spots	ellebeibedo, oi ildībot
squaie	eriisio
squint	possangu
squirrel	oirgabobo pl oigedassendaii
stamp (v. Imp)	eiroishu
stand (v. Imp.)	itashu {naitashi (sing.)} {megendaishi (pl)} Infin
stai	olāgirra pl elāgii
stay (v. Imp.)	taanyo, or toidona
steal (v. Imp)	etuburiōī, negibiiio (Infin.)
steinbock	mpaināss
stick	engudi pl mussidi
sticks (small)	loom pl elõõm
sticky	eyāda, or ebongishu
still	endegearada
stomach	ngoshogi pl ngõishoa
stone	ossont pl. soiitii
stoop (v. Imp)	engoiroma
strangle (v.)	tagoia
striped	geri
stripes	csserat

stroke (v Imp)	tooshora
strong	egol
stumble (v Imp)	atarŏiı
stump	engobē pl engoben
suck (v Imp.)	errana, eıtanag (Infin)
suckle (v Imp)	endaanga, or endaduagı
sugaı-cane	elleropat
sun	ngolong pl. ngolong
sunrıse	elebua ngolong
sunset	eraduı ngolong
sure	ıolo ossubadı (lıt to know well)
surround (v Imp.)	tamanaı
Swahılı people	elashomba, enganjura, or lorrıda
swallow (v Imp)	toıorjoı
swear (v Imp)	etamoro, negedek (Infin)
sweat	engengınyeret
sweep (v Imp)	tooro
sweet	emello
swell (v. Imp)	etejer, or eırēıı
swım (v. Imp)	eborrngaıe
swıng (v. Imp)	ıugo
sword	olalım pl lalıma
syphılıs*	ngaıouln

T

table	enaııa pl. enarıaı
taıl	orıgıdoıngaı pl eırgıdonga
taıl-pıece (waırıoı's)	orıgebessı pl. ıırgıbıssenı
take away (v. Imp.)	ıodomo oı endau (Infin), naıdau
take care of (v. Imp)	ıngorāī
take ıt	engo
talk (v. Imp.)	toojo
tarantula-spıder	engollopa
taste (v. Imp.)	enyoıayora
tattoo	orııngeııandus
teach (v Imp.)	keawtagem
teaı (v. Imp.)	tobolossa
teaıs	oırgıe pl. eııgıo
teeth (two fıont upper)	lalalegıshıa

* Literally "god knows " The Masaı had no knowledge of syphılıs untıl it was ıntroduced amongst them by the Swahılıs.

teeth (back)	eldagiligih
tell (v. Imp.)	tiagi, najogi (Infin)
ten	tomon
ten times	katitin tomon
testicles	ellderege
thank you	aāsi (lit an expression of delight)
that	lido, or ainyo
their	ejanggari
there	iddie
these	kolo
they	eninji
thick	sabuk
thief	olaburon, or ossūnguroi pl essenguru
thigh	engubiss pl engobessin
thin	rongai
thing	ndoki pl ndogitin
thirst	engorrei
thirteen	tomonoguni
thirty	ossom
thirty-one	ossomobbo
this	elde, or enā
thorn	orrkigui pl eirēgēgo
thorn tree (black-)	ollongossua
those	leguwa
three	ūni
thrice	katitinuni
throw (v Imp)	ondoirai, nauanga (Infin)
thumb	moiriukitok, oi oirkimojinu sabuk
thunder	egeiug ngai
tick	oiiomashere or masheri pl. ellemashei
tickle (v. Imp.)	ingitigito
tidy (v. Imp)	endobera
tight	teriesha, or teene
time	ngatitin, or ngatijin
tired	enauari
tobacco	orrgumbau
today	taāda
toe	orrkimojinu pl iirkimojik
tomato (wild)	endulele
tomorrow	taaiisere
tongs (large)	orramēt
tongs (small, for pulling out hair)	orrbutet

tongue	orienējap pl. ingejapa
tooth	ollālaı pl. lala
tooth-brush	engege
tooth-hole (bottom jaw in centre fiont where 2 teeth are always extracted)	embwāda
toitoise	olōīguma pl ollōīguma
touch (v Imp.)	ūngutugutı
trade	engınyanga
tiail (v. Imp.)	engoirtodai
trap	oiieshet pl. oiiesheta
tread upon (v Imp)	tāgedo
tree	oldanı pl. elgieg
tiee (baik used for quivers)	ollokıdong
tiibe	elōshon pl olōsho
tiumpet	emoworr (lit. horn)
trunk (of tree)	engobē
trunk (of elephant)	engaiıa (lıt. aiıı)
tiuth	esseba
try (v. Imp.)	enenanga
turn (v Imp)	engorrnajı, embellegenia
turn iound (v. Imp)	belegenia
tuitle	olōīguma
twelve	tomon are
twenty	tıgıtıım
twenty-one	tıgıtum obbo
twice	kātaie
twins	ellemāwu
two	arı, or are
two hundred	ıp arı

U

udder	oirigena pl. ellgiē
ulcer	olldododaı
uncle	engābo
under	ngop, or aborı
understand (v Imp.)	etoliıgu
unearth (v. Imp.)	tuduru
uphıll	ndigın
urine	engolac
use (v. Imp.)	issiashuii

V

vagina	ngumu or engwali
valley	orromoti pl. emotiok
vegetables	mbene
vein	engoň pl. engonya
very	ossūbati
village	engangiti pl. engang
village (warriors)	emanyata pl emanyat
virgin	engebaigen
voice	egossol, or elduelu
vulture	oilomotonyi pl. elmotonyi
vulture (white)	orrgŭleria pl elgelengweni

W

wait (v Imp)	ndashu, naanyo (Infin)
Wakamba	luungŭ
wake (v. Imp)	enyo
walk (v Imp.)	alolo, or enguiana
wall	essondai pl essondā
want (v. Imp)	aiu, naiu (Infinitive)
war	endiore pl endiona
war-cloth (warrior's)	enanga
warrior	elmorian pl lamorani
warrior (probationary)	naiseologunia pl esseologunia (lit shaven head)
war-song	olloiburri
wart-hog	olbitirr pl elbitiru
wash (v. Imp)	aisoja, naijoja (Infin.)
water	ngare
water-buck	olomālu pl ellemaloni
waterfall	ngare naruga
wealth	olganisis
we	eĕog, or iog
well	eloreshu, or ongēsumet pl erigesumeti
well (to be)	egolbiero
wet	eshell
what	ainyo, or iya
what for?	ainyo?
what is this?	ainyĕna?

M G.

what sort?	ainyo?
when	ānu
where	koıē
whetstone	engıı
which	koıe
whiskers (animal's)	elbabıt enoıet
whisper (v Imp)	engōmengōm
whistle (v. Imp.)	essōleshu
white	eboıı
who	enaıana
wholly	boōgı
why	ainyo
wild	ındım
wild dog	cssuyan
wildebeeste	oııngat pl. eengatı
wind	essıısıu, or ngıjāpı
wind (to make)	ejegātı
window	ellusıe pl. ellusıet
wings	naıbuku
wipe (v. Imp.)	tuduııu
with	alu, or nabo
woman	ngoıraıon pl ngoıroıok, teım of oppıobııum
	engıtok pl. engıtua, polite foım of addıess
	essıengegı pl. essıengegın, polite foım of addıess
	endagıle, addıess to young woman
	endamonon, pıegnant woman
woman (old)	koko
womb	sabu
wood (used for bellows)	lobōnı
work	engıas pl engıaset
workmen	elgunūno
worm	allaııogaı pl lāıoga
wound	ıngıbonōī pl ıngıboıo
wrinkles	engelat ossısın
wrist	erıobwada, erıobat ngaıına

Y

yam	olaıboırıborri
yawn	naıımin
yellow	nguıo
yes	aıyeı oı aneııyı

yesterday	ngole
yonder	elleeda, or nyedia
you	iye
your (sing.)	enino
your (plural)	eninyi

Z

zebra	eloidigo pl. eloidigoisho

CAMBRIDGE: PRINTED BY J. AND C. F. CLAY, AT THE UNIVERSITY PRESS.

Lightning Source UK Ltd.
Milton Keynes UK
UKHW020659200421
382299UK00005B/417

9 781376 002676